THE PRIDE
OF
AGGIELAND

THE PRIDE OF

AGGIELAND

HOMER JACOBS

PHOTOGRAPHS BY
KEVIN BARTRAM
AND
GLEN JOHNSON

To my dad, who took me to my first Aggie football game.
I was hooked then, and I'm still hooked now.

—Homer Jacobs

THE PRIDE OF AGGIELAND

For information contact:
Silver Lining Books
122 Fifth Avenue
New York, NY 10011
212-633-4000

Silver Lining Books and colophon are registered trademarks.

Editorial Director:	Barbara J. Morgan
Editor:	Fred DuBose
Editorial Assistant:	Emily Seese
Design:	Richard J. Berenson
	Berenson Design & Books, Ltd., New York, NY
Production:	Della R. Mancuso
	Mancuso Associates, Inc., North Salem, NY

Library of Congress Cataloging-in-Publication Data is available on request.

ISBN 0-7607-3257-4
ISBN 0-7607-3767-3 Deluxe edition

Printed in the United States of America

First Edition

TO SET FOOT ON THE TEXAS A&M CAMPUS is to step back in time. From the presence of the Corps of Cadets to the century-old traditions that form so much of the fabric of the school, Aggieland is as nostalgic as it is patriotic.

And yet the school that first resisted change from its all-male, military heritage has transformed itself into a large and dynamic university. All the while, Texas A&M has maintained and nurtured its identity as one of the most spirited campuses in the country.

In an unsettled world, Texas A&M is the perfect counterpoint to negativity and cynicism. To anyone who may wonder where honor and goodness have gone, I say come to College Station.

To visit with some of the venerable former students of A&M is to relive a time when pride and dignity, camaraderie and loyalty, were the basis for everyday living.

Countless military heroes have come through the ranks of the Corps of Cadets and fought courageously in our country's wars. We also have heroes who have starred on the football field. John Kimbrough, the burly back from Haskell, Texas, helped the Aggies win the school's only national championship in 1939. John David Crow won the school's only Heisman Trophy in 1957 when the commanding presence of Paul "Bear" Bryant led the Aggies out of the football drought of the 1950s.

From the days of coach Emory Bellard in the 1970s to the Jackie Sherrill era of the '80s—and finally to the R. C. Slocum generation of today—Aggie fans have been treated to some extraordinary football seasons. The glory years of 1975, 1985, and 1998 will be replayed in the minds of the maroon faithful forever.

While the pageantry of a Saturday afternoon football game in College Station creates incredible enthusiasm on the A&M campus, tragedies like the Bonfire collapse of 1999 and the terrorist attacks on America have strengthened the Aggie spirit even more.

Times have changed for all of us. Thankfully, the essence of Texas A&M has not.

Homer Jacob

CONTENTS

GEORGE BUSH

Dear Friends of Texas A&M University:

I am very proud to be associated with Texas A&M University. Placing the George Bush Presidential Library and Museum at A&M just seemed like the right thing for Barbara and me to do. The spirit, pride, traditions, and overwhelming love of country that Texas A&M represents follow so closely everything that my family and I believe in.

One reason my Library is there is because of the Aggie values, the Aggie spirit. Meet with the enthusiastic, patriotic, caring students and faculty of this place and you'll feel refreshed and renewed. That's why Barbara and I spend as much time at the Library as we possibly can.

Another reason for putting the Library at A&M has to do with the military. Over the years, Aggies have provided great service to the Armed Forces of our country. Patriotism abounds at A&M. Who can ever forget the "Red White and Blue Out" that followed the tragedy of September 11, 2001. That outpouring of patriotism that filled Kyle Field said it all.

I admire this school's fine values, strong academics and, of course, those incredible fighting Texas Aggies. This is a special place, and all Aggies have so much to cherish and be proud of.

I am glad to see the essence of the university so well portrayed in *The Pride of Aggieland*. This book is a colorful ode to the unique bond that students, former students and fans have with this one-of-a-kind university. There's plenty of history and football in the book, but it's really more than that. It's about the essence of Aggieland and all that the school represents.

I wasn't an Aggie way back in my own college days, but I am now.

George Bush
Forty-first President of the United States

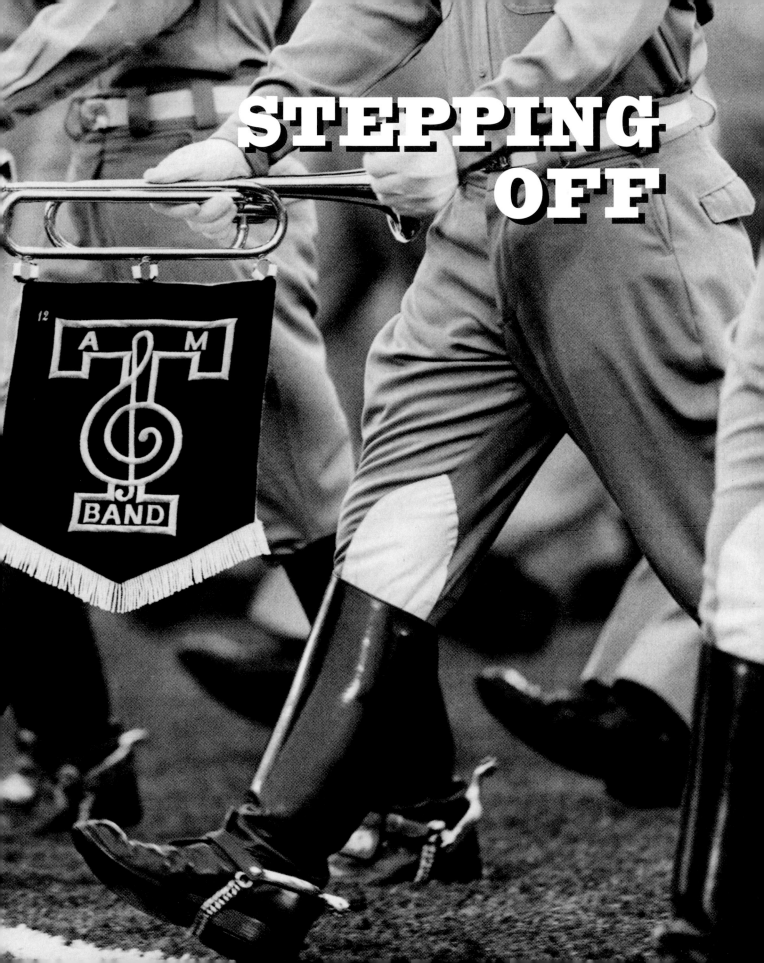

STEPPING OFF

Texas A&M University is almost unrecognizable from its beginnings as a remote land-grant college near the banks of the Brazos River.

THE TRAINS STILL RUMBLE IN AND OUT of College Station, timekeepers for a timeless place. The color of Cadet khaki is still glimpsed amid the sprawling live oaks that shade the campus, and the jingle of the senior spur still resonates from the old quadrangle as routinely as another rendition of reveille. The familiar dome of the Academic Building rises in the center of campus, and aging dormitories like Walton and Hart halls live on as comforting landmarks.

But Texas A&M University, the first public institution of higher learning in the state of Texas, is almost unrecognizable—in the physical sense, at least—from its beginnings as a remote land-grant college near the banks of the Brazos River in central Texas. Since those sleepy days, few universities in the United States have undergone such a quick and amazing transformation.

Birth of the Corps

Opened on October 4, 1876, the Agricultural and Mechanical College of Texas was to be a bastion for the common man, a place where anyone of any means could aspire to an education. Its small campus consisted of no more than a few buildings spread across a flat plain of dust and newly planted trees.

When the state constitution declared that funds from the sale of public lands would go toward the building of the college, there were already plans on hand to build a large, broad-based academic institution with an arts and sciences curriculum. But early lawmakers had decided that the University of Texas at Austin would handle that role, with A&M relegated to agricultural and mechanical studies.

In fact, though it opened its doors a few years before the University of Texas did, A&M was to be considered an annex to UT, and the Texas Constitution never amended that law. Merely a gentleman's agreement existed to keep A&M under its own umbrella. Only when oil was discovered on UT's public lands in 1923 did A&M succumb to the notion of being a branch of the University of Texas. That year, the Permanent University Fund (PUF) was established, and A&M fought

1885
* N. Wipprecht

Early Field Artillery at Texas A. and M. College
The Cannon Came from Civil War Artillery

In 1885, Aggies went through artillery drills as a part of campus life. But it wasn't until Lawrence Sullivan Ross arrived as school president in 1891 that military training became compulsory.

hard for a third of the royalties. The Aggies received their share, but the partnership between the two schools went no further. "We're part of UT for one day every year," former A&M president Jack Williams would say, ". . . when they split the PUF."

While A&M was the first public institution of higher learning in Texas, its mission was undefined. Was it to be merely an agricultural institution, or a school more like the soon-to-open University of Texas in Austin? It was all-male and all-military, but no law or handbook ever drew up such a mandate. Should it remain that way? It was not until the 1891 arrival of the school's new president, Lawrence Sullivan Ross, a former two-term governor of Texas, that A&M found its way and began to establish its extraordinarily distinctive identity.

It is no exaggeration to say that Ross saved the Aggies. Right before he came, there was even talk of shutting the school down as UT began to rise. But Ross had a vision. The man who had served not only as governor but in the Texas Rangers—the state's legendary law-enforcement outfit—declared that Texas A&M, an agricultural and mechanical college up to then, must have military training as its central mission. And so began a whole new era.

In this outpost 90 miles from Houston and a million miles from the ordinary, the Aggies soon became known more for their spirit and camaraderie than for their science curriculum or library. The credo of

Did You Know?

In the early 1900s, the official school colors at Texas A&M were actually red and white. But almost 30 years later, when an order went out for football jerseys, the supplier made an error: The jerseys came back maroon. Faced with the dilemma, an athletic department official decided to keep the jerseys because red was the color chosen by so many other colleges. And the rest is history, as they say.

Sounding Off

"Over the years, a reputation evolved among parents that if you wanted a good, straight place where your kid could go to a school that would make a man out of him, work him hard, and get him a good education—and if you were looking for a no-frills kind of deal—this was the place to do it.

"I've heard stories about some of the guys from the classes before the 1920s who were helped financially by the school. The obligation they felt was that once you were out of college and on your feet, you would help the school so it could help some other less fortunate guy. Aggies helping so that other Aggies could be helped developed into the idea that Aggies stick together. To me, that's fundamental to the whole philosophy of A&M."

—*R. C. Slocum,
head football coach since 1989*

the Corps of Cadets was "training leaders of character and competence for service to nation and state." True to form, Cadets followed strict military life: They rose at sunrise to bugle play, marched down Military Walk to the campus chow hall, and drilled for war in the afternoons. In between came classes.

The Cadets began to bond and, in turn, to foster traditions—some born out of boredom and bull sessions, but most derived from respect, loyalty, and values that came with a conservative, military lifestyle. Many of those traditions dealt with everyday life in the Corps dorms, while others centered on football games. Still others, like the solemn Silver Taps (first Tuesday of each month) and Aggie Muster (April 21) ceremonies—which honor those Aggies who have died during the past month or year—were military traditions that helped differentiate A&M from any other school in the country.

The spirit of Aggieland—A&M's longtime, identifying intangible—was building, later to mythical proportions. The reasons for such burgeoning pride can be traced back to the lineage of this long maroon line of farmers, ranchers, oilmen, and military heroes. They came to the little college, where they were welcomed without reservation, in hopes of receiving some kind of education on meager means. Many students worked for the school, often handing out uniforms or shaping the Corps of Cadets' famed senior boots as a way of paying their tuition. A strong work ethic was emphasized, and a firm bond was formed between student and institution. Suddenly, A&M seemed more than just a place to study agriculture and mechanical engineering.

With the A&M Corps of Cadets living and marching and eating together, the Aggies became one big family. Sometimes they were teased because of their uniforms, the lack of women on campus, and the scarcity of bright lights in the village of College Station. But the family was tight, and the jokes would cease when the Aggies answered their calls to duty, fighting for America in some of the biggest battles and conflicts the world has seen.

Almost 20,000 Aggies fought in World War II alone, and the list of A&M heroes is long and distinguished. There is the story of James Earl Rudder—the school's famed president from 1959 to 1970—leading his Army Rangers up the cliffs at Omaha Beach on D-Day to secure a key German post. There was the courage of Ray Murray, a regimental commander in Korea who earned three Navy Crosses for bravery. And Floyd Carpenter, class of '77, was the lead bomber for the first sortie flown over Baghdad in day one of Operation Desert Storm.

A retired corps commandant, Maj. Gen. Ted Hopgood, says the depth of respect for A&M's military past is genuine. And deserved. More than 225 former members of the Corps have achieved the rank of general or admiral in the armed forces. And although service in the Corps calls for no military obligation, more officers are commissioned

The Corps of Cadets falls into formation in 1906. Before World War I, the uniforms worn by the Aggies were of gray wool, not khaki.

The Aggies marched to chow in 1920. Today, the 2,000 members of the Corps of Cadets eat all of their meals together in Duncan Dining Hall, on the south end of campus.

Seniors in the Corps, identified by their signature leather riding boots, prepared for World War II in the shadow of the Academic Building.

into all branches of the military from Texas A&M than from all other schools, apart from the military academies.

Hopgood calls on his Cadet days often. He remembers when, as a brigadier general stationed at the Pentagon in the early 1990s, a three-star general chewed him out for some spotty work. The episode hardly frazzled the hardened Hopgood.

"I said, 'Yes, sir, I got that. What next?' He kind of looked at me like, 'Hey, you weren't fazed by that and were ready to go on.' He calmed down, and we went on. It was a reaffirmation of the Aggie way of doing things."

That confrontation would serve Hopgood well. He was on overnight duty at the Pentagon on the night that Iraq invaded Kuwait in a move that precipitated the Gulf War. Along with another Aggie on duty that night—Brig. Gen. Hale Burr—he helped put into motion all the dynamics of a full-scale war. Hopgood and Burr increased the defense condition (DEFCON) of the United States from level 5 to 2, changing the alert status of the nation's military in minutes. With the two Aggies' recommendations, the White House froze all Iraqi assets in the banks of the United States, turned a carrier and battleship group around at sea, and placed the 82nd Airborne and 2nd Marine Division on their highest alert.

"Even for an Aggie who was a non-varsity athlete," Hopgood added, "there is an appreciation for performing under pressure—of having a lot of eyes on you and realizing you have a lot more depending on you than the score on a scoreboard."

A Spirit Like No Other

In the years following the end of World War II, life at A&M was once again unsettled. As the university tried to find its way, it would suffer setbacks both academically and athletically. The Aggies, their faculty, and their former student base were at odds over whether to continue compulsory membership in the Corps of Cadets and whether to allow women into the school.

Athletically, the Aggies were suffering on the hallowed ground of a football field. Previously, the football team had given up a combined total of only seven points in the seasons of 1917, 1919, and 1920 and won the national championship in 1939. They also had winning years under legendary coach Paul "Bear" Bryant, but Bryant left the Aggies following the 1957 season to coach his alma mater, Alabama. After his departure, A&M suffered through nine straight losing seasons. And perhaps most ignominious of all, from 1940 to 1975, the Aggies beat their arch rival Texas just three times.

What contributed to A&M's decline on the football field? First of all, the advent of World War II drained A&M's student-athlete pool in

Maj. Gen. Ted Hopgood

"Even for an Aggie who was a non-varsity athlete, there is an appreciation for performing under pressure—of having a lot of eyes on you and realizing you have a lot more depending on you than the score on a scoreboard."

Opposite page:
Before each home football game, *the Corps Commander leads his units around Kyle Field in the traditional March-In.*

17

Sounding Off

"I think that because of the Texas A&M experience—we were smaller, we were different, we were military, we were agricultural, and we were located in a remote area—there was an inward turning of everybody to what's here. What we found when we looked inward was each other . . . we found other Aggies. Spirit would be the catchall phrase, but spirit does not begin to explain it."

—Maj. Gen. Ted Hopgood, U.S.A (Ret.), class of '65

the 1940s. Then, questionable coaching hires from 1948–53 (Harry Stiteler and Raymond George), an NCAA probation during the Bryant era in 1955–56, and the rise of Texas as a national college football power all took their toll. In 1967, Coach Gene Stallings, one of Bryant's former players, led A&M to a surprising Southwest Conference title. But from 1956–75, the Aggies won just three conference championships.

These may have been disquieting times for Texas A&M, but they were still years when the Aggies pulled closer and closer together. The trophies may not have been piling up in the athletic offices, but student-body groups and alumni bases could feel the almost spiritual undercurrent that swept through the campus. While the 1960s and early 1970s found the country at odds with itself over the Vietnam War, and antiwar fervor grew stronger and stronger, a yearning to remain fiercely loyal and traditional—often despite the ridicule of others—tugged at the Aggies. Students were becoming accustomed to a common battle line: Us against them. *We are the Aggies, the Aggies are we*—a familiar verse of the school's alma mater, "The Spirit of Aggieland"—rang truer than ever.

Instead of traditional cheerleaders, Texas A&M boasts five male Yell Leaders. They direct the crowds at Kyle Field with various hand signals and body motions.

The spirit and fortitude built during an era when it would have been easier to run with the mainstream—burning flags rather than waving them—would lay the foundation for the Aggies' hard stance of taking on the world. Along with the military way of doing things, the spirit dating back to 1909 (Bonfire) and 1922 (the 12th Man) helped start many of the famous traditions that are associated with Aggieland: Silver Taps, Muster, Midnight Yell Practice, Yell Leaders, and Reveille, the Aggies' American collie mascot.

While the University of Texas was known for its

Reveilles VI and VII team up for a photo opportunity. The first Reveille (her jacket shown at right) was named in 1931 after she barked nonstop at the sound of reveille.

Freshmen in the Corps, just like all students, show their support for the Aggies by standing throughout the game, a part of the fabled 12th Man tradition.

Women now make up almost half of the student body at the former all-male, military school. The Aggie Hostesses (above) serve as ambassadors for the football team, while many women (right) now occupy leadership positions in the Corps. Former interim university president Dean Gage (below) adjusted to the coed way of life in the 1960s.

protests and its parties, A&M, with its allegiance to male bonding and a belief in God, country, and football, began to separate itself from other universities in the region.

"First of all, you have this extreme loyalty," A&M historian David Chapman recalls. "Then you have the group thing. And there's a mystical belief in the traditions, which have taken on an almost religious fervor. There's a feeling of wanting to be connected to the past. Today the school has a lot of kids who are from broken homes. But to them and everyone else, A&M is like granite: These people are your brothers and your sisters."

Not until A&M would admit women, make the Corps of Cadets noncompulsory, and aggressively change its academic attitudes did the school finally transform itself into one of the nation's premier universities.

A&M Arrives

And the image of Texas A&M? In the 1960s, when the military way of life was everything and the enrollment barely topped 8,000 students, the image was of a school in need of a major makeover.

Not until A&M would admit women, make the Corps of Cadets noncompulsory, and aggressively change its academic attitudes did the school finally transform itself into one of the nation's premier universities. In the 1970s and much of the 1980s, A&M was the country's fastest growing university. In just over three decades—from 1970 to 2000—the school grew threefold, enrolling 36,652 undergraduate students in the fall of 2001. It was the largest undergraduate number in the country.

"I don't know of any school that has undergone such a dramatic change," says Jerry Cox, a 1972 graduate and one of the school's most influential former students. "If you had told me in 1970 that one day we would have 44,000 kids here, that 50 percent of them would be women, and that the Corps would represent only 5 percent of the student body, I would have said it was very unlikely that the value system, the camaraderie, the closeness, and the traditions could last. But for some reason, they have."

In 2001, A&M was ranked eighteenth among the best public universities in the country by a prominent national publication. It also received a coveted invitation into the elite Association of American Universities.

The Aggies had truly stepped off.

THE WOMEN OF AGGIELAND

GEN. JAMES EARL RUDDER'S PRESENCE is felt everywhere on and around the Texas A&M campus. His statue glistens in the shadow of Rudder Tower at the center of a school he helped transform, and Rudder Freeway sideswipes the towns of Bryan and College Station.

But for all of his accolades as a military hero and steadfast university president (1959–70), perhaps Rudder's most telling and lasting act came during a routine recess of an Association of Former Students (AFS) board meeting on January 25, 1964. It was during that coffee break that Rudder approached the board's president, John Lindsey of Houston, and handed him a brief handwritten note on a torn piece of paper. The gist of the note was poignant and piercing: Admit women on a full-scale basis.

"You're joking, Earl," Lindsey recalled saying. "And I handed the note back to him. He said, 'I'm not joking. I'm just not.' "

Although a few women—the wives of students and daughters of A&M faculty—had been allowed to take courses from the time the school was founded, the idea of a full-fledged coeducational institution had been fought tooth and nail. The Aggie armor had been dented the year before, when the board of directors voted on April 27, 1963 to give more standing to the wives and daughters of A&M faculty and staff—and to admit "qualified women" to graduate programs and the school of veterinary medicine as well. The outrage that followed that landmark decision had echoed not only through the halls of Aggieland but beyond.

A stream of letters—all the more passionate because, in the same year, the school's name had been changed from Agricultural and Mechanical College of Texas to Texas A&M University—flowed for weeks into Rudder's office. "Congratulations," one former student wrote. "Ordinarily, it takes much longer to destroy 92 years of tradition." An A&M graduate from Roanoke, Virginia, even tore his diploma in half and mailed it to Rudder with a note: "I have removed my Aggie Ring and returned my diploma. The name change and the coed thing is more than I can stand." Sixty Cadets on campus shaved their heads in rebellion against even limited

James Earl Rudder

admission of women, and Rudder had to calm the disgruntled student body with a speech—heard by 4,000—at G. Rollie White Coliseum.

John Lindsey knew that those reactions would be small potatoes compared to the feelings stirred up by a resolution to fully admit women. But he also knew that Rudder—a man of vision, and with plenty of moxie to boot—was in no mood for wasting a good opportunity to move his school forward.

When the AFS meeting's recess was over, Lindsey announced that one more resolution had to be voted on before adjourning. "Boy, there was a lot of chatter in the room," Lindsey recalls. "I talked a little bit about how serious this was, and pointed out that General Rudder was present." Then came the shock:

"General Rudder gave me a resolution to admit women all the way. He wants and needs it. Gentlemen, this is the best thing for our university—and now I'm going to call on a vote."

A landmark decision by the board of directors in 1963 allowed for the admission of women to Texas A&M. In 1974, women were allowed to join the Corps of Cadets.

Lindsey remembers the scene: "I said, 'Those in favor say aye,' and there were some ayes. 'All opposed say no,' and there were a lot of noes. But I said 'The ayes have it,' and that was that." He then adjourned the meeting. Many of the men were "yelling for [another] voice vote and a ballot vote," but Lindsey refused to budge.

The AFS may have passed the resolution, but they pulled no punches when it came to letting their real feelings be known. They inserted a statement that the admittance of women would happen "without approval, endorsement, or the blessings of the association." Despite the misgivings of the AFS's rank and file, Rudder had all he needed for the board of directors to give the green light to women. Just like that, an iron-fisted president of the university and an equally bold president of the Association of Former Students had changed A&M's makeup forever.

There was some early resistance to the idea of coeducation at A&M, as this "questionable" page layout in the 1964 yearbook clearly shows.

From Backlash to Growth

The repercussions of the resolution to admit women to A&M would be felt profoundly into the next century. And in a personal sense, the decision was a costly one for reformers like Rudder and Lindsey.

Rudder—who had been convinced that coeducation was the best way to save A&M by none other than his good friend and political confidant, Lyndon B. Johnson—had to contend not only with demonstrations on his manicured front lawn but also with students' uncertainty about the future. Lindsey, who had graduated only 17 years before, had to look into the steely eyes of the old Ags—eyes that were filled with anger and even tears.

In retrospect, however, women were admitted just in time. From the end of World War II until 1965—when the school went coeducational and the Corps of Cadets was no longer compulsory—Texas A&M was falling out of favor with prospective students as military training lost its appeal. While state schools like UT, Texas Tech, and the University of Houston were growing rapidly in enrollment, A&M enrollment barely passed the 8,000 mark in 1962.

If the decision to allow women into the university had not been made, most Aggies agree that A&M would have gone the way of the long gray lines of the southern military academies: Small, distinguished, stately . . . but in the end, archaic.

With women now a part of A&M, new questions arose: Would Aggies be able to sustain their traditions, which were based on an all-male, all-military culture? Would A&M become just another run-of-the-mill school with a fading ROTC program? Or would the admittance of women mean updated degree plans and a better academic reputation?

A&M would eventually change its physical plant by building female dorms and adding women's rest rooms to classroom buildings. But the women who trickled into the school in the late 1960s had no choice but to live off-campus, since the first female dorm wasn't built until 1972.

Another indication of the slow pace of change was the academic catalog's absence of any mention of coeducational opportunities until September 1971. In 1963, the limited enrollment of women had attracted only 183 females, and the number of women at the school grew by just 1 percent each year through 1969.

"Admitting women was a huge change," says John Lindsey. "The women knew the student body didn't want them there, and they knew most of the Association of Former Students didn't want them there. I think it was pretty gutsy for the ladies to come anyway."

Sounding Off

"I was told by my adviser, Joe Townsend, that A&M had never had a female student-body president. But because I never felt any different at the school or thought that women didn't belong, I found that hard to believe. Besides, A&M was always such an open, warm place. What Townsend told me piqued my interest, so I got involved in student government and decided to run.

"When we were campaigning, I got some comments that A&M was just not ready for a female student-body president. But I always had a lot of confidence that this just wasn't the case—that if I was really the right person at the right time, it would happen, regardless of gender."

—*Brooke (Leslie) Rollins,*
class of '95

Women Make Their Mark

It was in the early 1970s that women began to really take to A&M, with one fourth (7,182) of the student body made up of women by 1975. In 1980, there were 12,207 women at A&M out of a burgeoning student body of 33,499. By the mid-1990s, the freshman classes were admitting more women than men, and of the 44,000 students on campus in 2002, 49 percent of them were female.

Like it or not, A&M had been reinvented, and the women students' enthusiasm would ensure that Aggies would remain Aggies—loyal to the Corps, the traditions, and the values that were ingrained generations before. If the Corps' Cadets were considered the keepers of the spirit, the women of Aggieland were the doting mothers.

In a monumental election that showed the full transformation of A&M from an all-male school to an all-encompassing one, A&M chose its first female student-body president in 1994. Brooke Leslie (now Brooke Rollins) would be the first of three female student-body presidents over the next eight years. Ironically, Leslie, a Future Farmers of America participant from Glen Rose, showed up on campus as one of her male counterparts might have 50 years ago—intent on advancing the agricultural way of life.

It wasn't until the end of her freshman year, after first having gone through a football season and then attending Aggie Muster in the spring, that Leslie realized how unique A&M was. "That was when I really got the fire to give something back to the school," she recalled.

Judy Franklin: An Aggie Pioneer

In the fall of 1964, controversy and cantankerousness swirled around the Texas A&M campus, after the board of directors had approved a resolution for the admission of women to the school in April of 1963. And while daughters and wives of professors and administrators had been admitted on a select basis (not on a four-year-degree plan), the 29 women who enrolled at A&M in 1964 would become the first class of coeds to leave its historic stamp on a university at the start of an incredible metamorphosis.

As former students howled at the idea of the full-scale admission of women to their beloved university, and as media swarmed around the campus, sniffing a good, sizzling story, 29 women took a chance as pioneers. The past had been shaped by Aggies, who, almost a century before, had arrived in College Station by train, on mules, or even on foot. The future of Texas A&M would be formed by daring women who would break down the barriers of tradition and a male-dominated college culture.

Judy Franklin was one of the "first 30," as she likes to call her classmates. As a native of Bryan, Texas, she was familiar with A&M and its unique yet narrow educational opportunities. But Franklin's dream was to pursue a degree from one of the top journalism schools in the country—either the University of Missouri or the University of Texas.

After pondering her future and coming to an agreement with her parents, Franklin decided to attend A&M for two years, gathering enough core credits to transfer to Missouri or UT to pursue a journalism degree. But once Franklin survived the first year at a changing Texas A&M—even with all the hoopla surrounding the arrival of women—she knew her calling was to become and remain an Aggie.

"It was definitely awkward, and there was a lot of trepidation on the part of women," said Franklin. "Almost every day there was some editorial or articles quoting former students who were opposed to coeducation. And I had heard freshmen in the Corps were told not to even look at coeds as they passed them on campus. That was coming from upperclassmen. By the spring semester, that had all changed because it was those same upperclassmen asking the single girls out on dates."

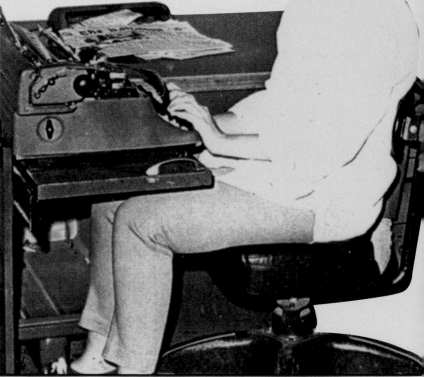

Judy Franklin, as a staff writer for The Battalion in her junior year, and today.

Indeed, the makeup of the A&M campus was quickly changing, and both the men and women were beginning to accept—and even relish—the idea of an integrated campus. For years, an Aggie's social life had depended on train schedules and the willingness of women from Texas Woman's University in Denton to travel. The socializing with the sister school, however, would soon be replaced by interaction with coeds on the campus in College Station.

In fact, as Franklin recalls, the relationship between the male and female students improved with each passing day. Although mild teasing between the students existed in day-to-day college life, many of the early obstacles between men and women were hidden in the teacher-student relationships.

Many professors had chosen A&M to teach because of the male-only, military lifestyle. Women suddenly were invading their classrooms, and some of the old academicians didn't appreciate it.

Franklin remembers one unyielding economics professor who taught his class using football terminology as his bridge of communication. A biology professor—in a classroom of 200 males and Franklin—pulled down a chart to discuss the intestinal tract of the human form. Of course, the anatomy was that of a woman.

"How does one react? You just chuckle embarrassingly, just as the guys did," Franklin said. "The guys were there for me, and they were embarrassed for me. I found them very protective. I had a D in another class and some of the guys tried to talk the professor into changing the grade, but he refused."

Franklin, today the executive director of

development for the A&M System's Health Science Center, jumped headfirst into leadership roles during her student days, hoping to build her social and educational opportunities. Even at Bonfire cut site—a tough, male domain where students would cut and gather wood for the annual red-hot yell practice before the Texas football game—Franklin would distribute doughnuts to the hardworking Aggies. She became known as A&M's first official "Doughnut Dolly," the precursor to the Cookie Crew members who have contributed to Bonfire morale with food and drink over the last two decades.

While the dress code for women was strict in the late 1960s (dresses and skirts were required) and women's rest rooms weren't plentiful right away, Franklin says A&M students and administrators—particularly school president Earl Rudder—were determined to deal with the new changes as the university tried to enhance its academic standing and image around the state of Texas.

Judy Franklin was the first female graduate (1968) from A&M with a journalism degree. She received confirmation that she helped pave the way for A&M's tremendous growth as a university when, at a Muster ceremony in 2002, a former Corps of Cadets member approached her with open arms.

The man was a senior at A&M when Franklin first stepped foot on campus.

"Do you mind if I give you a hug?" he said. "I just really liked you then and I wanted you to know how much I appreciated you."

By the 1970s, *life on the Texas A&M campus was changing in ways that an earlier generation of students couldn't have imagined. The enrollment of both male and female students was booming— so much so that A&M became the fastest growing university in the country.*

Like so many of the women at A&M, she was transfixed by the school's traditions and Aggie football.

Women's growing involvement in campus activities propelled them into leadership roles that no one could have envisioned even 10 or 15 years before. Schuyler Houser was elected 2001–02 student-body president, and three of her four vice presidents were women. That same school year—and the next—the presidents of the Memorial Student Center (a memorial for all the Aggies who gave their lives in the armed forces, and the hub of student activities) were women. Throw in the plethora of female directors of Fish Camp (freshman orientation in the summer) and Aggie Band members, and the women of Aggieland are everywhere. As for the Corps of Cadets, it took the lead by allowing women to participate in 1974—much earlier than any military academy in the United States.

Leadership roles for A&M women were taken up by former students as well. Carri Baker Wells (class of '84) became the 2002 12th Man Foundation president, while the Association of Former Students elected Glenda Mariott (class of '79) to the president's chair in the same year. Both were firsts for the two fund-raising organizations.

Schuyler Houser says she can't imagine Texas A&M without women on campus, upholding the traditions that have shaped the fabric of everyday life in College Station. "It's interesting to see the way women adapt to the traditions," she says. "The girls are out there at Bonfire, Midnight Yell, and at football games. Just like the men, they stand the whole time—so I think they've risen to what those traditions demand of them."

The women of Aggieland not only helped build the enrollment

of Texas A&M but also sparked a growing reputation in academic circles. Admitting women meant improving and increasing degree programs and taking them beyond military training and agricultural sciences. Yet all the while, A&M kept marching to its unique beat, pounding with history and tradition.

As students walk across Texas A&M's modern, bustling campus, a wide variety of dress is in full view. Twenty-two hundred members of the Corps of Cadets still walk to class in full uniform, and seniors in the Corps strut with their signature brown boots. For the 42,000 other students, known as non-regs, casual wear is the norm. Pockets of Greek life mean that fraternity and sorority T-shirts dot the classrooms. But for every Tau Kappa Epsilon T-shirt or Future Farmers of America jacket that flashes by, the colors and letters most prevalent in Aggieland are maroon and white and A&M—just as Earl Rudder had envisioned, just as he had hoped.

Sounding Off

"If Earl Rudder hadn't had the courage to stand up and say we're broader and bigger and more diverse than this, we probably would have ended up a small regional military academy.

"A&M was a school looking for its way. It was the height of the Vietnam War, and it was the counterculture of the '60s vs. the soldier. The changes introduced in the years that followed the admission of women played an immensely positive role in the broadening of the scope of A&M. It extended our values to more than just those people who happened to wear a uniform and tote a rifle."

—*Jerry Cox,*
former president
of the 12th Man
Foundation

FOOTBALL: THE STAGE FOR THE SPIRIT

From the first time the Aggies took up football in 1894 to the present, when over 85,000 fans fill Kyle Field, Aggie football has been at the center of a very tight circle.

IN THE CLAUSTROPHOBIC DORM ROOMS of the old campus, the ambience was one of linoleum and humidity. Factor in the remoteness of College Station and the fact that back then women dotted the Aggie landscape only when the trains rolled in from Denton (home of Texas Woman's University) and the scene was not all that exciting.

Still, Aggies sensed they were in a special place. Maybe it was the military way of doing things in the Corps of Cadets. Or maybe it was the traditions, the camaraderie, and the school spirit that made the Aggies believe there was no place like Aggieland.

While the pride was intense inside the maroon fences, Texans had little exposure to the Aggie way of life. From the 1930s through the '50s, the social circles of Dallas and Houston were not filled with Aggies, but with big money graduates of SMU and TCU as well as the sheer mass of Texas Exes. To add insult to injury, Texas's new interstate system bypassed College Station. Unless you had good reason to visit desolate Brazos County, you didn't bother.

So how were the Aggies—bursting at the seams with loyalty and pride—going to show the rest of the world what it had been missing? Easy: Give them six Saturdays every autumn—six cram sessions of Spirit 101 on a college football afternoon. Football may rule the rest of Texas, but at Texas A&M, football fever reaches an all-time high.

From the first time A&M took up football in 1894 to the present, when over 85,000 fans fill Kyle Field, football has been at the center of a very tight circle. Yet the school's football exploits have never been likened to those of perennial powers Notre Dame, Alabama, and Nebraska. Instead, A&M's football history has been loaded on the back end, with one sixth of the school's all-time victories (617) coming in the last 10 years.

Despite that, the pageantry of the Corps marching into the stadium, the students standing during the whole game, and the big brass and precision play of the Aggie Band have created an atmosphere that few

In 1894, Texas A&M played its first official football game—against the University of Texas in Austin. The Aggies lost to the Longhorns 38–0.

schools—if any—have been able to duplicate. Yes, winning games is important, but for the Aggies, football Saturdays are more than that: They're a time not only to revel but to reveal a spirit like no other.

"Game day, in particular, embodies the spirit that underlies the whole A&M tradition," says Jerry Cox, an Aggie football regular who watches games from his 50-yard-line suite at Kyle Field. "We have a value system and an ethic of acceptance. We are not bashful about stating that we value things such as honesty, loyalty, and camaraderie. It's on game day that we get to manifest those attributes in a collective way. It's more than just about being in attendance. It's about being an integral part of the spirit."

Retired Maj. Gen. Ted Hopgood, the Corps of Cadets commandant from 1996–2002, grew up in North Dakota, and he still remembers

Texas A&M football now plays to overflowing crowds at huge Kyle Field. The Aggies were longtime members of the Southwest Conference before joining the Big 12 Conference in 1996.

Sounding Off

"At A&M, there was a chip on everybody's shoulder because we sensed that people thought of us as a second-best university. From the urban centers and other campuses, that was the message these rural kids were getting. But not only were we proud of football, we reveled in it. In fact, with our traditions, we may have tried to become even more different than anyone else."
—*archivist David Chapman, class of '67*

a cold Thanksgiving afternoon watching Texas A&M play Texas in the mid-1950s. Televised sports were new back then, and Hopgood recalls the camera panning from atop Kyle Field, over the oak trees that cover Spence Park. "I can remember it like it was yesterday," says Hopgood. "There was something about this intense rivalry between the two schools and what was going on that was captivating. I thought, 'Wow, these people are serious.'"

The Ultimate Furlough

In the school's early years, football was instantly attractive to A&M Cadets. As an emotional outlet after hours and days of military training, three hours inside a football stadium—in a state where football is a way of life—seemed like the ultimate furlough.

But football hasn't always been an easy adventure for the boys on the Brazos. In fact, as much as it helped create a passionate link between the fans and their school, the sport has teased and taunted Aggies for decades.

Football began at A&M as a club sport, and the school's archives have references to its debut in 1892 and 1893. College football at the turn of the 20th century was more rugbylike, with scrums instead of huddles and more kicking than passing. After Walter Camp, a former Yale player and coach in the late 1880s, popularized the game national-

In 1902, Texas A&M claimed its first victory over Texas, 11–0. Although no conference yet existed, the Farmers were proclaimed Champions of the Southwest.

Did You Know?

A common myth has it that the Aggie's first football game was against Galveston's Ball High School. In fact, the school's name was a misnomer: "Ball High" was a hodge-podge of players of all ages from the Galveston Sports Association. The Aggies went up against them on Thanksgiving Day of 1894, but the first official A&M game took place later that same year. The game was with A&M's future rival, the University of Texas, which dealt the Aggies a 38–0 loss.

By World War I, *Texas A&M was an SWC powerhouse. The 1917 team won the school's first conference championship with an 8–0 record.*

The Battalion, *the school newspaper, covers a game in 1911.*

ly with a more defined set of rules and scoring, three Aggie men decided the game of football should become the campus's main exercise outside the marching that took place on the drill fields. With others' help, these pioneers—Charley Herndon, Art Watts, and coach Dudley Perkins—organized A&M's first official football team.

A&M fielded football teams from 1894 to 1908, but the sport really began to take hold when Charley Moran took over as head coach in 1909. Moran, who had coached at Vanderbilt and Tennessee, and had umpired baseball in the National League, was a no-nonsense—and win-at-all-costs—football coach. A&M went 29–3–1 in Moran's first four years of coaching.

But there was a fly in the ointment: Moran was accused by many schools of cheating—or at least fielding less-than-ethical teams. Gamblers were involved in those games, knowing that A&M often recruited ringers from the Haskell Indian Institute to beef up team rosters. The Indian players from Haskell (near Abilene, in West Texas) would arrive on campus on Thursday nights, taking advantage of the state rule that allowed a player to suit up for a team if he had gone to classes on a campus for just one day.

Charley Moran took more than a little liberty with the rule, ultimately drawing the ire of his competitors—most notably those from Austin. The University of Texas took a firm stance and refused to

play Moran's teams from 1912 to 1914 because of his shenanigans.

Ironically, the Southwest Conference (SWC) was created in 1915 to put a stop to the misguided ways of certain teams, A&M included. A&M professor and athletics council chairman Edwin J. Kyle, for whom Kyle Field is named, was one of the original proponents of the SWC, the same league that would dissolve 80 years later because of financial drop-offs and years of—of all things—cheating. (At one time or another, five of the SWC's nine schools were put on some kind of probation in the 1980s. The league finally folded in 1995, with four former SWC schools—including A&M—merging with the Big Eight to form the Big 12 Conference in 1996.)

After Moran's departure in 1915, Dana X. Bible took the Aggies to six conference championships in his 11 seasons as head coach. But after the 1928 season, Bible would defect to the University of Nebraska—and later to Texas. The Aggies were unable to duplicate Bible's success until Homer Norton hit the recruiting jackpot in the spring of 1937. A&M rose to the top of college football with the 1939 national championship, but the Aggies dropped off the college football map in the 1940s—thanks in large part to decimated rosters as the Aggies headed to World War II. Only a peach-fuzzed group of 16- and 17-year-olds, nicknamed the Kiddie Korps, kept the football buzz alive at A&M in 1943, with a surprising 7–2–1 record and Orange Bowl invitation.

With the effects of the war still lingering through the 1940s, coupled with the onset of the Korean War, life was more about survival than football on college campuses, including football-loving Texas A&M. Things turned around in 1954, with the arrival of Paul "Bear" Bryant as head coach. But while Bryant gave A&M new hope for its football program, his quick exit to Alabama after just four years depressed the Aggie community all over again.

Although the school would win just one SWC title in the 1960s, it once again burst onto the national scene in 1975 after a 20–10 win over No. 5 Texas. A&M jumped to 10–0 and the No. 2 ranking in the country. But hopes for a national championship were lost the following weekend on a cold day in Little Rock, when A&M fell to the University of Arkansas Razorbacks 31–6. The Aggies would finish the year with a 20–0 bowl loss to Southern California.

Glory Years

The glory years of Aggie football wouldn't come until the 1980s and 1990s. Yet through all of the down years, probation years, and war years, Aggie football remained a constant draw to students and fans. It still beckons each fall like a cold beer at the famed Dixie Chicken saloon—College Station's most famous watering hole since 1974.

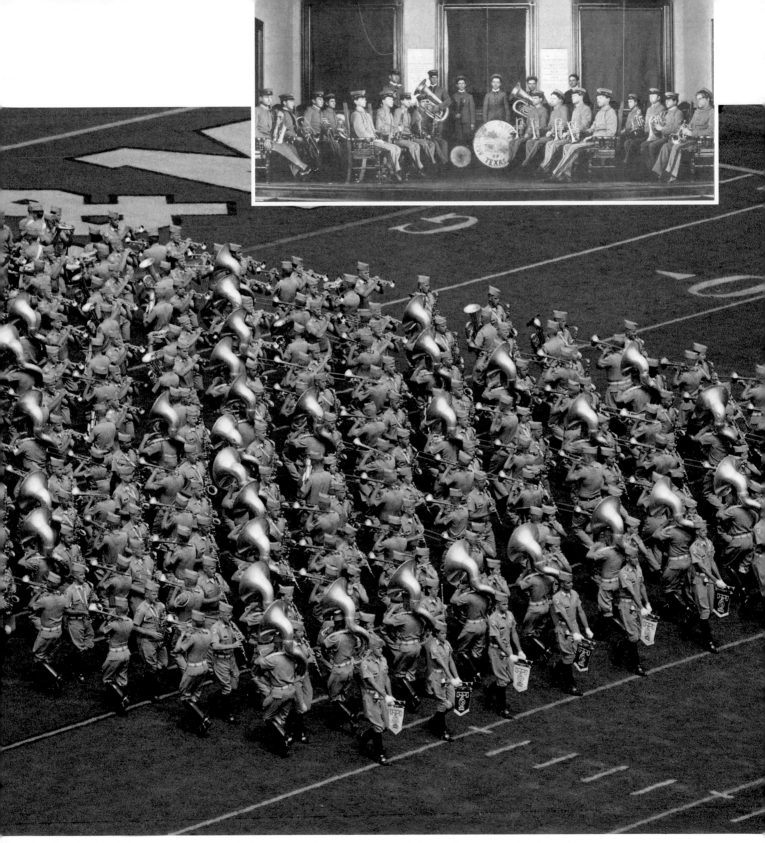

The football field provided a grand stage not only for the football players but for the Aggie Band. First formed in 1894 by Joseph Holick, the Band was made up of just 14 members. Today, the Aggie Band's elaborate halftime routines are performed by almost 400 men and women.

In 1904, Edwin Jackson Kyle fenced off a section of land with barbed wire to set aside a space for athletic contests. In 1905, he bought lumber for a fence and bleachers, covering the cost with a personal note.

In 1906, a covered grandstand from the Bryan fairgrounds was purchased and moved to Kyle Field. It provided a seating capacity of 500.

It was also football that gave birth to the proud Aggie Band, A&M's pulsating, 400-member group of Aggies to the core.

The Band began as a musical lead dog to take the Cadets to chow and back, and was hardly the marching machine it has become today. When it was formed in 1894 (by Joseph Holick, the original maker of the senior boots) it numbered just 14 members. It later grew to approximately 400, none of whom attend A&M on a music scholarship.

For a rousing military marching band that wanted to perform before more than just the Corps of Cadets at a military review, there was only one stage to play on: Kyle Field—and it was now bigger and bolder than ever.

The field's original shacklike grandstands, built with $312.63 worth of lumber in 1907 (paid for with Edwin Kyle's own money), have been overhauled through the years. They became a one-deck horseshoe, followed by double- and triple-deck expansions. The latest stadium addition, in 1999, saw the north end zone expanded—at a cost of $33 million—to push Kyle Field's seating to 82,600 permanent seats. An enclosed, 100,000-seat colossus seems possible by 2010.

If Kyle Field has undergone a multitude of changes, so has the tradition-bound university that surrounds it. Yet for the Aggies, the return to campus on a fall Saturday reminds them that things can stay the same, that tradition can remain intact. The yells that ring down from the

top of the third decks are much like those that resonated 50 years ago. While the five male Yell Leaders may have varied their hand signals slightly over the years (one thing that hasn't changed is the male-only policy for Yell Leaders,) both present and former students follow the routine like a well-orchestrated chorus line.

In 2002, R. C. Slocum, A&M's longtime head coach, said that he still felt goose bumps on Saturday mornings in the fall even after 30 years of coaching on the A&M campus. And he still watched with pride as Aggie families unloaded for the weekly tailgate party, with grandfathers wearing their colors on flat-billed caps and grandsons wearing theirs on caps flipped backward.

And as the famous Corps of Cadet poem, "The Last Corps Trip," proudly proclaims: *The boys still march in behind the band.*

Kyle Field *has become the state's largest football stadium, with crowds of over 85,000 now commonplace. A state record of 86,125 fans squeezed into the arena for the 1999 game against the University of Texas.*

1939
RISING FROM THE DEPRESSION

*The **stark** Texas A&M campus in 1922*

As scarce as money and food were around the dusty campus, victories on the football field were even harder to come by.

ON THE STARK TEXAS A&M CAMPUS OF THE 1930s, the spirit of Aggieland and the fortitude of the country were being tested like never before. The Great Depression had sapped the nation's finances, and for the Aggies, football was no longer king. Basic survival took top priority.

A&M had always taken in boys from the rural and meager side of society. Cadets worked as mess hall waiters or pressed uniforms at the campus laundry to help earn their keep. But these tough times pushed the Aggies to new depths of hardship. Football players, for instance, lived four to a room in "project houses" at the south end of the stadium. Care packages from parents provided the essentials—canned goods and corn bread—not frills.

And as scarce as money and food were around the dusty campus, victories on the football field—the Texas Aggies' sacred ground of pageantry and escapism—were even harder to come by during that difficult decade of the 1930s.

The glory years of the teens and '20s had drifted into history. Under head coach Dana X. Bible, the Aggies had won 36 games and lost only three from 1917 to 1921. The 1917 team gave up zero points in an 8–0 season, while the 1919 squad outscored its opponents an incredible 275–0 to gain consideration by many as the top team in the land. Bible would lead the Aggies to Southwest Conference titles in 1921, 1925, and 1927, dazzling A&M football fans as powerfully as the Charleston riveted good-timers in the dance halls of the pre-Depression South.

A&M football began to flounder as the 1920s closed and Bible headed to the University of Nebraska and later to Texas to steer their football programs. From 1929–1933, coach Matty Bell's Aggies won just 20 games in five years, and his successor, Homer Norton, did little at first to revive the Aggies' football fortunes.

Football losses mounted—as did financial debt. The Great Depression was over, but depressing times were socked in over this central Texas campus.

The Aggies' Top 40 Chart

Homer Norton had been hired in 1934 in hopes of resurrecting the football program within five years. By the end of the 1936 season, those hopes had been teased with an eight-win season. Still, Norton knew that a banner recruiting season was probably the only way his career and the program were going to be saved in the long run.

Norton needed help in a big way, and it came in the form of Lilburn "Lil" Dimmitt—a football trainer by trade, and an emergency recruiter by necessity. Dimmitt had coached a variety of sports at A&M, including basketball, track, and baseball. His charge as a member of the football staff was to come up with a list of the top players in the state for Norton to recruit.

Forty players emerged on Dimmitt's list in the spring of 1937. By the fall of that year, 37 players on that list had shown up on the Texas A&M campus in search of a scholarship and a better way of life. But both aspirations were tenuous, at best.

While Dimmitt's recruiting prowess had landed the players, paying for their schooling presented a major obstacle. The athletic department already was in default on interest and payments on a $210,000 bond to help build Kyle Field a decade earlier.

It was wealthy electrical engineer and A&M alumnus Bert Pfaff

In the early '30s, enthusiastic Aggies gather for Midnight Yell Practice on the steps of the YMCA Building.

45

John Kimbrough *became a legendary running back for the Aggies, leading them to the 1939 national championship.*

who came to the rescue, and just in time. A&M needed a $25,000 loan to cover the cost of the 37 football scholarships, and Pfaff strong-armed his own bank in Dallas, threatening to pull his $400,000 personal account if the money wasn't made available to the Aggies. The bank buckled, lent A&M the money, and laid the foundation for future football glory.

Among the "Wanted 40" whom Dimmitt and Norton secured were All-State quarterback Marion Pugh of Fort Worth North Side High School; center Tommie Vaughn of Brownwood; fullback/guard Marshall Robnett of Cooper; and a churning fullback from Haskell, John Kimbrough. Tulane had originally signed Kimbrough, and the 210-pounder showed up on the New Orleans campus as a midterm high school graduate. But after a position switch to tackle and a rift with Tulane's head coach, Red Dawson, Kimbrough was cut from the team. He headed home to Texas, finding solace and a scholarship in College Station.

For the Cadets and their beloved football team, the dark clouds were dissipating. Kimbrough was coming—and so, too, was Texas A&M's greatest single season in over a century of college football.

Undefeated, Untied, and Unaccustomed to It All

Conference rules dictated that the 37 freshmen who stepped onto the A&M campus in 1937 could not play in varsity games until they were sophomores. They could practice with the upperclassmen, though, and those practice sessions became legendary. As cannon fodder for the varsity, the blue-chip prospects—nicknamed the "Blue Boys"—toughened and hardened the junior and senior classes to the point where the A&M team was showing marked progress.

In 1938, the Aggies barely reached the .500 mark, turning in a 4–4–1 record. But a close 7–6 loss to Texas and a 27–0 blanking of Rice to end the season stirred the fire for the off-season and summer of '39.

With the excitement over the 1939 season came expecta-

Did You Know?

Admittedly, the Aggies didn't play the toughest of schedules back in 1917 and 1919, considering that tepid teams like Trinity and Dallas University—now UT at Dallas—showed up on the dockets (the Aggies humiliated Dallas 98–0 in 1917). But there's no questioning Texas A&M's dominance during that period, under coach Charley Moran. In those two seasons combined, A&M did not give up a single point, outscoring its opponents 545–0.

Seventy-five years later, a group of college football historians calling themselves the National Championship Foundation would declare the 1919 Aggie team one of the four best teams of that season, along with Notre Dame, the University of Illinois, and Harvard. But a banner year though 1919 was, Texas A&M recognizes only the official Associated Press national championship title of 1939.

tions, as well as worries over a note due on the stadium. It was imperative that this team win and win big. The time was right for Edwin Kyle, chairman of the athletics council, to give the Aggies the locker-room speech of a lifetime. And he did. Right in the bowels of the stadium named for him.

Kyle's rousing speech, which made it clear to all that the entire future of Aggie football was at stake, did the job. The Aggies stormed out of the meeting and into the 1939 season, with a contest against a solid Oklahoma A&M team as the opener. A fired-up Texas A&M squad ran away with a 32–0 victory.

Of the 37 recruits, six had become starters by the '39 season opener and 12 were filling in as backups. By the time A&M had beaten Shreveport's Centenary College and then national powerhouse Santa Clara from California, eight of the starters had been Blue Boys. In those days, guys not only played both offense and defense but nearly all of the allotted 60 minutes.

And who should be leading the unbeaten Aggies—and playing 550 out of a possible 600 minutes in 10 games—but John Kimbrough, his knees high-stepping through defenders like pistons cranking in the boiler room of the Titanic.

Now a junior running behind players like Vaughn and alongside stalwarts like Pugh, All-America captain Joe Boyd, Robnett, and Thomason, Kimbrough became the region's most dominant offensive player—and perhaps its toughest. After working the ranches of West Texas and surviving the daily grind of the Corps of Cadets life, he wasn't about to let an opposing defense cause him any problems.

"In my day, the coach told us, 'Boy, if you can't block that man or do this or that, then get on the highway and get back behind that mule and chop that cotton,' " Kimbrough would say. "They would take your scholarship away that same afternoon."

Riding on the broad back of Kimbrough, the '39 Aggies began to steamroll through their schedule. After a 20–6 drubbing of 1938 national champion TCU, the Aggies would record four shutouts over the next five games, including a 20–0 whitewashing of Texas before 40,000 at Kyle Field to close out the regular season. And the numbers the Aggies had piled up in the 10-game season were both record-breaking and startling.

En route to the 10–0 record and a No. 1 national ranking, the Aggies shut out six opponents and allowed only 18 points—the

Sounding Off

"When Kyle gave us his speech, he told us that there was a note due on the stadium. He also made it clear that Republic Bank was giving us a lot of trouble about it. What I remember very well is what he said about our ability to be a good team and to help the school financially. Let's just say he kind of put the pressure on us."

—Howard Shelton, reserve center on the 1939 team

1939 Season Scores

Texas Aggies	Opponents
32–0	Oklahoma A&M University
14–0	Centenary College
7–3	Santa Clara University
3–7	Villanova University
20–6	Texas Christian University
20–0	Baylor University
2–0	University of Arkansas
6–2	Southern Methodist University
19–0	Rice Institute
20–0	University of Texas
14–13*	Tulane

*Sugar Bowl Game of January 1, 1940.
Season record Won 11, Loss 0, Tied 0; Total Score 212–31

47

1939 Texas Aggie Football Team Statistics
10 Games not including the Sugar Bowl Game

	Texas Aggies	Opponents		Texas Aggies	Opponents
Games Won	10	0	Yards Intercepted Passes Returned	400	159
Touchdowns	30	2	Number of Punts	90	114
Points after Touchdown	18	1	Average Distance of Punts	37.1	37.2
Field Goals	0	1	Number of Punt Returns	57	42
Safety	0	1	Number of Kickoffs	43	10
Total Points	198	18	Average Distance of Kickoffs	48.2	52.0
First Downs	118	54	Number of Kickoff Returns	10	38
Yards Gained Rushing	1682	664	Average Distance of Kickoff Returns	25.0	18.1
Yards Lost Rushing	173	249	Number of Penalties	62	40
Yards Gained Passing	1029	348	Yards Lost on Penalties	576	351
Net Gain Rush and Pass	2538	763*	Fumbles	14	16
Forward Passes Attempted	166	175	Own Fumbles Recorded	7	4
Forward Passes Completed	70	48			
Forward Passes Had Intercepted	15	28			
Percent of Passes Completed	.422	.274			

* The average of 76.3 yards per game, rush, and pass set a new national record for defense. It also worked out to 1.71 yards per play run.

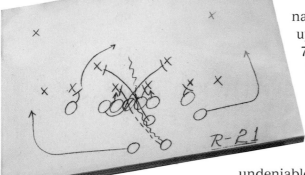

Shown above
is the original playbook for the 1939 Aggies, who finished 11–0 with a 14–13 victory over Tulane.

nation's best mark for points allowed. A&M's defense gave up just two touchdowns all year and allowed an amazing 76.3 yards per game. That total defensive mark remains an NCAA record, and probably will never be broken. A&M's stout defense also gave up just 1.71 yards per carry, also a feat that will likely remain untouchable.

Kimbrough finished the season with 475 yards rushing on 143 carries, scoring 10 touchdowns. But it was his hard running style, Hollywood good looks, and undeniable presence that began to shape his superstar status, both on and off the field. "He's the greatest football player in the world," Norton bellowed to one state newspaper. "And you can put my name on that with a picture."

With Texas A&M and Tennessee both unbeaten and untied in the

1939 Texas Aggie Football Team Individual Statistics

10 Games not including the Sugar Bowl Game

Ball Carriers

Player	Times Carried	Yards Gained	Yards Lost	Average Gain
Thomason	15	67	0	4.44
Conatser	62	308	37	4.37
Moser	83	396	46	4.22
Kimbrough	142	503	28	3.35
Jeffrey	21	73	5	3.25
Pugh	46	146	11	2.93
Price	16	73	5	3.25
Audish	3	8	0	2.67
Force	4	10	6	1.00
Spivey	11	25	12	1.18

Punters

Player	Punts	Total Distance	Average Punt
Wood	1	48	48.0
Wesson	4	191	47.8
Thomason	1	41	41.0
Conatser	46	1675	36.4
Moser	37	1303	35.2
Force	1	34	34.0

The '39 Aggies recorded six shutouts, including a 20–0 win over Texas at Kyle Field.

Passers

Player	Passes	Completed	Yards	Intercepted	Percent Completed
Pugh	84	43	468	10	.512
Kimbrough	2	1	30	0	.500
Price	47	20	430	3	.426
Moser	14	3	62	0	.214
Jeffrey	19	3	39	2	.157

Pass Receivers

Player	Passes Caught	Yards Gained	Player	Passes Caught	Yards Gained
Herb Smith	17	237	Sterling	2	24
Buchanan	10	149	Spivey	2	11
Thomason	9	161	Bama Smith	1	46
Moser	9	148	Cowley	1	19
Conatser	6	107	Price	1	11
Kimbrough	5	43	Joe White	1	6
Jeffrey	3	32	Duncan	1	6
Dawson	2	29			

The 1939 Aggies, coached by Homer Norton, remain A&M's lone national champion in football. Several members of the team went on to successful business careers, while John Kimbrough starred in two movies and was a national pitchman for the L&M cigarette company. All but two members of the squad earned their college degrees—and of the 51 players who eventually married, only two would end up divorcing.

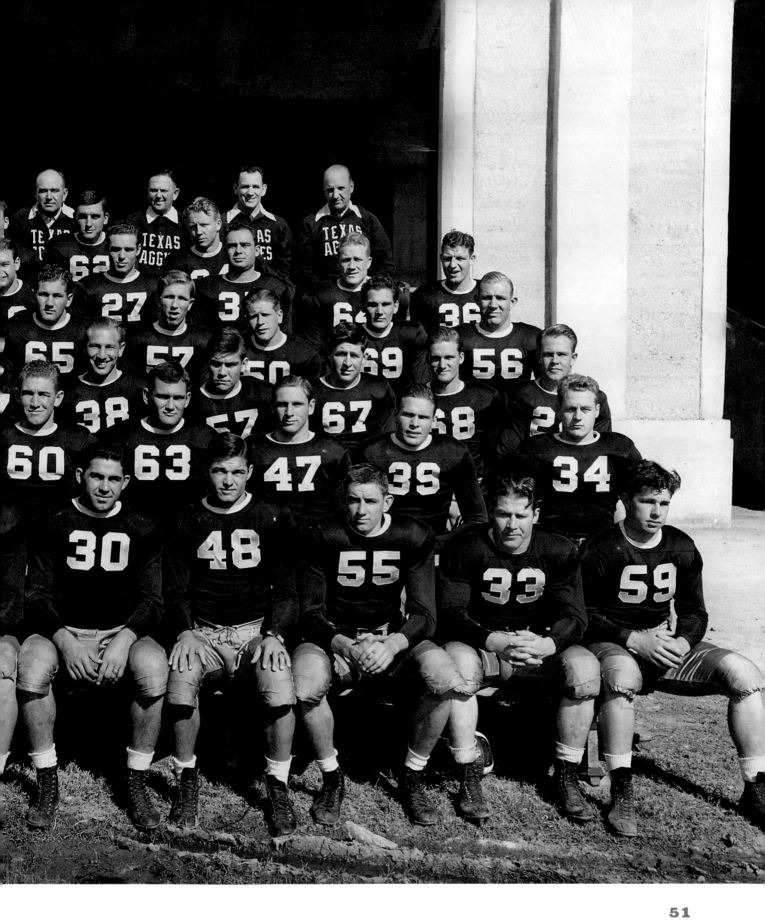

John Kimbrough's bruising style captivated a nation. Yet he finished fifth in the Heisman Trophy voting in 1939 and second in 1940.

1939 season, the Cotton Bowl Classic in Dallas was hoping to land a New Year's Day game for the ages. A group of Dallas bankers and businessmen were ready to ante up $85,000 per team to secure the dream matchup. But the Aggies balked at the starting time of the game, which was set for evening. A&M wanted an afternoon game to allow for warmer conditions, and Tennessee wasn't ready to commit to the Cotton Bowl until it had beaten the Plainsmen of Alabama Polytechnic (later Auburn).

Instead, A&M took its next best offer, accepting an invitation to play fifth-ranked Tulane in the Sugar Bowl. A group of kids from Texas farms and ranches were about to take on the private-school guys from New Orleans. The Agricultural and Mechanical College of Texas, the school that almost closed down at the turn of the century and nearly lost its football program to foreclosure, was one game away from winning it all.

A Classic in New Orleans

Despite the fact that the Texas Aggies were unbeaten and ranked No. 1, life around the 40 buildings on campus went on much like always: reveille in the morning, Silver Taps at night. Sure, the Aggie way of life was energized by the success of its football program, and a decade of dust and debt was over in the state of Texas. Yet there was hardly any statewide or national hyping of the Aggies, who, except for a trip to California to meet Santa Clara, had played a regional schedule.

It wasn't until the Aggies took the field before a standing room–only crowd at Tulane Stadium that the nation began to take notice. The electricity inside the 73,000-seat stadium was so palpable that the writers from the nation's newspapers could hardly contain their enthusiasm: "Goose pimples tall as giant asparagus sprouted," wrote Flem Hall of the *Fort Worth Star-Telegram*.

Once the ball kicked off, Kimbrough pounded the Green Wave for an early touchdown and a 7–0 lead. And although Tulane rallied for a 13–7 lead, the murmur in the press box and stands was that it was just a matter of time before A&M flexed its muscles—before Kimbrough bullied his way into the end zone for the game winner.

After a 70-yard drive in the fourth quarter, Kimbrough took a lateral from Herbie Smith and barreled into the end zone to tie the game at 13–13. Charles "Cotton" Price then kicked the all-important extra point for the dramatic victory.

It was the first time all season that a team had scored in double

A standing room–only crowd of 73,000 greeted the Aggies in New Orleans's Sugar Bowl. Texas A&M rallied from a 13–7 deficit to clip the Tulane Green Wave, 14–13.

digits against the stingy A&M defense, and some national correspondents called this college football game one of the most fiercely contested they had ever seen. "Only a truly great team could have beaten Tulane on that day," *Chicago Tribune* reporter Arch Ward declared. "You couldn't escape the impression that you were watching one of the greatest groups of athletes the game has seen . . . and the greatest piece of football flesh this writer ever saw. He [Kimbrough] is too much football for one team to stop."

At game's end, the Aggies weren't giving much thought to whether they would be crowned national champions. That hadn't been their primary goal during the season, nor were newspapers around the country giving much attention to the team from College Station, Texas.

Not until the Aggies returned to their hotel, the Roosevelt in downtown New Orleans, did they taste the spoils of their rocketing success. With a touch of panache that perhaps only a New Orleans hotel could serve up, the A&M players were told to step onto an elevator two at a time. A hotel waiter wearing white gloves and carrying two champagne bottles escorted each pair of Aggies up to their respective floors.

Even then, it wasn't until the team was heading back to College Station on the train that anyone mentioned the possibility of being named national champions. The Associated Press had declared the Aggies No. 1, but news was slow to follow the maroon and white on their way back home.

As team center J. Howard Shelton recalls, "Somebody came to the back of the train and said, 'You know, we're national champions, we're the No. 1 team in the country.' We said, 'Really . . . are we?' "

In reality, the Aggie players had lived day-to-day during that 1939 season, bonding in the project houses and dorm 12 of the Corps of Cadets living quarters. They were satisfied just to have endured the long, hot practices when John Kimbrough's knees seemed to never stop pummeling their bodies at the line of scrimmage.

Kimbrough's running style in '39 was no doubt eye-catching, but he still finished with just 475 rushing yards, dropping him to fifth in the Heisman Trophy voting that year. But more important to Kimbrough, the Aggies were unanimous national champions. A&M would keep the hot streak going into 1940, winning 19 straight games during the two seasons, losing only in the 1940 finale to Texas, 7–0. Kimbrough, who most thought was the most dominant player in the 1940 season, would finish an agonizingly close second in the Heisman voting to Michigan's Tom Harmon.

Despite all of the team glory and Kimbrough's successes during their championship run, the Aggies of 1939 will tell you, to a man, that this team was more about camaraderie and loyalty than first downs and toss sweeps. It was about being tough guys during lean times and Aggies all the time.

A football from the 1939 season may have lost some air, but the memories of that special year remain vivid for the players lucky enough to have been a part of it.

Despite all of the team glory and Kimbrough's successes during their championship run, the Aggies of 1939 will tell you, to a man, that this team was more about camaraderie and loyalty than first downs and toss sweeps.

A Bond That Never Breaks

The 1939 Aggies remain Texas A&M's lone national championship team, and large maroon letters hang from the second deck of Kyle Field to signify that unforgettable accomplishment. Yet the living players from the '39 squad talk more about what kind of men that team turned out than the kind of football players it produced.

Yes, John Kimbrough and co-captain and kicker Cotton Price later played some pro football. But when World War II called on the '39 Aggies, most of the players—Kimbrough included—entered the service. Sadly, some players—like receiver Herbie Smith, one of the stars of the Sugar Bowl, and triple-threat back Derace Moser—were killed in accidents in Air Force training for the war. But for those players who survived World War II (several earned prestigious military honors), many came back to the United States to start successful business careers and large families.

Avoid Registration
Waiting by Paying
Your Fees Early

The Battalion

Student Tri-Weekly Newspaper of Texas A. & M. College
Official Newspaper of the City of College Station

Friday on WTAW:
"Aggie Clambake"—4:30
Battalion Newscast—5:15

VOL. 39   PHONE 4-5444   COLLEGE STATION, TEXAS, TUESDAY MORNING, JAN. 30, 1940   Z725   NO. 46

National Champs Feted As Honors Come To Aggieland

Bank Nite

Bowl Champs Claim Trophy

Bowl and Board Officials Preside

Individual Presentations Made to 1939 Champions

By Bob Nisbet

Saturday night's Sugar Bowl victory banquet was "Bank Nite" for fifty-four Texas Aggie football players.

Heroes in the eyes of the cadet corps, they received expensive watches, mammoth trophies, costly leather jackets,—to mention but a few of the innumerable awards. Gold and silver were everywhere in evidence.

Of course the most important trophy of all was the Sugar Bowl that was set on a special pedestal in the center of the banquet room for all to observe.

The first awards were made by Coach Homer Norton immediately following Dr. Law's speech of the evening. Norton first called the names of the boys on the squad who did not letter, then asked and got a hearty round of applause for these boys who did so much work for so little credit.

Thirty-one men on the squad qualified for and received T medals and/or bars, according to the number of letters earned. With the medals went blankets and leather jackets to the following men: Bill "Rock" Audish, Joe Boyd, Roy Bucek, Bill Buchanan, Bill Conatser, "Big Dog" Dawson, Bill Duncan, Henry Hauser, Charlie Henke, Marland Jeffry, Jack Kimbrough, John Kimbrough, Derace Moser, Ernie Pannell, Walemon "Cotton" Price, Marion Pugh, Leo Rahn, John "Bubba" Reeves, E. Robnett, Marshall Robnett, Chi Routt, Martin Ruby, Herb Smith, Marshall Spivey, James Sterling, Jim Thomason, Tommy Vaughn, Earl Weason, Jo Jo White, Frank Wood, and team manager Jimmy Parker.

Cross-country team members also received their awards at this time. They are captain Micky Hogan, who got a T jacket and bar; Alec Walker, Gene Wilmeth and Gus Laney, who got medals.

The next announcement of awards was made by Charlie De Ware, coach of the Freshman team who presented numerals to the following players: Bando, Bearden, Boyd, Brewer, Bucek, Drake, Duncan, Ferrell, Knight, Kraras, Mac Nab, Minnock, Mitchell, Milholland, Pickett, Rankin, Sharp, Smith, Swank, Templeton, Thompson, Tullis, Voss, Webster, Wilson, Yarborough, Zapalac, and Zinick.

Willie Zapalac from Bellville was chosen captain of the freshman team, to receive for this honor a gift from the Aggieland Pharmacy of a pen and pencil set.

Joe Utay, chairman of the Athletic Committee on the Board of Directors, stating that he, himself had once made application in vain to the All-American committee presented two beautiful life-size silver footballs mounted on mahogany bases, with engraved silver plaques in front, to the team's two All-American players, Joe Boyd and John Kimbrough. In presenting the awards, Mr. Utay stated that the two boys had lived up to all the requirements set for All-Americans, and hoped they would continue to be All-Americans in later life. With the trophies, the award carried with it two free passes to each man for all future athletic contests held at A. & M.

It was at this time that John Kimbrough announced he had a gift to make. He then brought forth the football that was used in the Sugar Bowl game in New Orleans, inscribed with the names

(Continued on page 4)

"TROPHY DAY" CLIMAXES AGGIES' MOST TRIUMPHANT SEASON

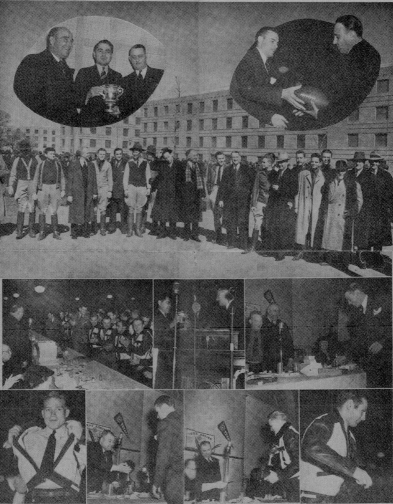

Above are shown the highlights of last weekend at Aggieland, as a group of leading officials of the New Orleans Mid-Winter Sports Association, which holds the annual Sugar Bowl game, visited A. & M. to put in its possession for a year the famed trophy, at the end of which time a duplicate will be given A. & M. for permanent possession.

At the top are shown in the new dorm area the Sugar Bowl officials with a group of prominent seniors who escorted them about the campus and in to dinner at the new dining hall. Herbert A. Benson, president of the association, declared during his visit that the sight of the cadet corps marching in to the mess hall to the music of the great Aggie Band was one of the most impressive sights he had ever seen.

Inset, left, Registrar E. J. Howell, member of the Athletic Council, holds the newly arrived bowl as Aggie head coach Homer Norton looks on happily. Benson stands at the right.

Inset, right, "Big John" Kimbrough presents the original football, inscribed with the names of the entire Aggie squad, to Bert Pfaff, ex-Aggie who presented the two best-blocker awards, during the course of the victory banquet Saturday night.

Center, left, Aggie grid stars at the speakers' table are overwhelmed with delight at master of ceremonies Col. Ike Ashburn's announcement of Jesse Jones' surprise gift of watches for all the lettermen.

Center, right, E. J. Howell, acting for the Athletic Council, accepts the Sugar Bowl from association president Herbert Benson, before the microphones of the Texas Quality Network in Guion Hall.

Below: (1) Joe Boyd dons his new fleece jacket. (2) Kimbrough receives his All-American silver football from the college, presented by Joe Utay, chairman of the Athletic Committee of the Board of Directors. (3) Boyd, after getting his All-American football, is presented by chairman E. M. Law of the Board, a permanent pass for two to all future A. & M. games. (4) Jim Thomason, another Aggie football great named one of the two best blockers, is awarded another of many gifts. (Both All-Americans received this honor.)

Program At Guion Hall

850 Attend Victory Banquet For Aggies

The great Aggie football team of 1939, undefeated, untied, and number one in the nation, hit the jackpot again Saturday night at the largest football banquet ever held at A. & M. honoring a team. Gifts, awards, and praises were heaped upon an appreciative group of boys whose smiles and blushes were many and frequent. Preceding the banquet, Registrar E. J. Howell, acting in the absence of Dean Kyle, chairman of the Athletic Council, officially received the Sugar Bowl trophy from members of the New Orleans Mid-Winter Sports Association.

Setting off the fireworks at 5 p. m. in Guion Hall, Col. Ike Ashburn following "Wildcat" and "Goodby to Texas" by Aggie Band, introduced over the Texas Quality Network to the state of Texas, Herbert Benson, president of the New Orleans committee, who spoke for a few minutes on the benefits of the present post-season game set-up in the nation. In his speech, Mr. Benson stated that he was most impressed with the great spirit shown by the corps. Then he turned to Registrar Howell and presented him the famous trophy to take in the name of the college and keep until another team is declared the Sugar Bowl Champion.

The Sugar Bowl trophy, a huge silver loving cup made in England and engraved "Texas A. & M. 14, Tulane 13", will be placed in the glass trophy case in the Academic Building to rest there until next New Year's Day when a duplicate will take its place to remain in A. & M.'s possession forever.

Regret was expressed by President Benson that the Sugar Bowl Association's vice-president and successor, Abe Goldberg, and also Warren Miller, past-president and founder, could not attend the ceremonies. However the following members of the committee did attend: Hap Reilly, publicity chairman; Fred Digby of the New Orleans Item-Tribune; Clarence Strauss, secretary of the committee; and Joseph David, treasurer.

Col. Ike Ashburn, at his best in jokes and wise-cracking, opened the banquet with the welcome words "Everyone please be seated." Then a larger-than-expected crowd of more than 800 football enthusiasts sat down to a feast of broiled tenderloin steak, French-fried potatoes, string beans and hot rolls, followed by a dish of ice cream covered with fresh strawberries. While the eating was in progress the Aggieland Orchestra provided a musical menu of popular pieces including among the numbers their own interpretation of "Goodby to Texas" and the increasingly popular "I'd Rather Be A Texas Aggie."

The program was opened with a telegraphed message from Dr. Walton in New York where he is attending a meeting of the Association of Land Grant Colleges; another from Bill Stern, NBC radio announcer and sports commentator; and another from Chester Munroe of the Southern Pacific Railway, all expressing their congratulations to the team and the coaches.

One of the best comments of the banquet was expressed by Colonel Ashburn about the same time explaining the general feeling of the crowd toward the past football season. Shakespeare put the words in his titles. "The past season," Col. Ike said, "was the achievement of our 'Midsummer Night's Dream'; it was 'Much Ado About Something,' and it was certainly 'As We Like It.'"

Further entertainment for the evening was provided by the Aggie Glee Club, introduced as "The A. & M. Men's Chorus." They gave three numbers, "God Bless

(Continued on page 4)

A Star Is Born

Perhaps no Aggie captivated a school, a state, and a nation like Jarrin' John Kimbrough did in the late 1930s and 1940s. Hollywood handsome and tough as boot leather, Kimbrough successfully made the crossover from athlete to national celebrity like no A&M product before or since.

After leading the Aggies to the 1939 national championship and finishing second in the Heisman Trophy balloting in 1940, the bruising fullback caught the eyes of the nation's advertising and entertainment industries as well.

Kimbrough signed an advertising contract with the Liggett & Myers Tobacco Company, and his dashing face made its way into magazine and newspaper ads and onto billboards.

"I was probably the most popular guy in College Station, because every week the Liggett & Myers Tobacco Company would send me a full case of cigarettes," Kimbrough told Rusty Burson for a feature article in *12th Man Magazine*, the official publication of A&M's 12th Man Foundation. "I didn't smoke, so I'd give them to all the guys that smoked at A&M. The only problem with me not smoking is that they had to paint a cigarette in my mouth [for the ad]. If you don't smoke, you don't know how to hold a cigarette."

Kimbrough also signed a contract with Twentieth Century Fox to appear in two western movies, *Lone Star Ranger* and *Sundown Jim*. Add in the American Football League contract he signed with the New York Yankees (the richest pact in the game, at $1,500 per game), and Kimbrough was capable of leading the life of the rich and famous.

But after suffering three heart attacks—his first at age 30—and serving in the military from 1942 to 1946, Kimbrough was content to lead a more secluded life in his West Texas hometown of Haskell (pop. 3,362). Along with his wife, Barbara, whom he married over 60 years ago, the 84-year-old Kimbrough enjoys the quiet life.

But the noise Jarrin' John created over a half century ago still resonates on the Texas A&M campus, where a street in his name shoots out from the shadows of the stadium he once transfixed.

"As far as I'm concerned, John Kimbrough is the legend of Texas A&M football," says A&M great John David Crow. "He's legendary not only because of what he did individually but also because he was the leader of the '39 team that accomplished something no other team at Texas A&M has ever done. Some sportswriters used to compare me to him when A&M was ranked No. 1 in 1957, but to me, there's no comparison. John Kimbrough is *the* A&M football legend."

Tommie Vaughn became one of Houston's premier automobile dealers, while Marion Pugh rose to become one of Bryan–College Station's most prominent construction magnates. (A street in Pugh's name winds through College Station's southwest side.) Howard Shelton went on to preside over several large banks in the state of Texas, and lineman Mack Browder held the title of vice president for administration at Dr Pepper.

But not all success was related to business: Of the 54 players on the 1939 squad, all but two earned their college degrees. And of the 51 players on the team who eventually married, only two marriages would end in divorce.

As for Kimbrough, the dashing, slashing fullback from Haskell capitalized on his fame and handsome face to become a national celebrity, Hollywood-style. He starred in two B movies, adorned billboard advertisements for cigarettes, spent one term on the Texas State Legislature, and was elected to the National Football Hall of Fame, the Texas Sports Hall of Fame, and the Texas A&M Athletic Hall of Fame.

In light of their success on the field, the 1939 season still befuddles some of the players to this day. After all, the Aggies never were really much of a ballyhooed bunch that season.

"It still just beats the hell outta me how we won the national title," says halfback Jim Sterling. "It was just one of those things that seemed destined to happen. All of us happened to be there at the right time and the right place."

For Howard Shelton, who has helped organize countless reunions and the presentation of a presidential endowed scholarship for academics from the '39 Aggies, the memories of that national championship season remain as vivid as ever. He can still smell the musty old project houses and feel the hits doled out from Jarrin' John Kimbrough. In his mid-eighties, Shelton never misses a home game at his beloved Kyle Field. As he stares up at the massive Zone, rising from the same spot where Edwin Kyle called on the Aggies to save the stadium and the football program, the goose bumps rise . . . perhaps, as the Fort Worth sportswriter wrote, as tall as "giant asparagus."

"Every time I enter the campus, I get a very funny feeling in the bottom of my stomach," says Howard Shelton. "It's about that camaraderie that we, as a team, had. I've been around the world twice and shook every bush, but the very best friends I have today are the friends on that football team."

In light of their success on the field, the 1939 season still befuddles some of the players to this day. After all, the Aggies never were really much of a ballyhooed bunch that season.

1956
THE BITE OF THE BEAR

Someone needed to stir things up.
Some larger-than-life figure had to
rekindle the Aggie spirit. That someone
arrived in the form of a striking
six foot three football coach for the ages.

IN THE FEEL-GOOD DECADE OF THE 1950S, when college life revolved around Elvis and a sleek new Chevrolet, the students at the Agricultural and Mechanical College of Texas were searching for their own king.

The Aggies' beloved football team was sliding in the post–World War II years, winning only 23 games from 1947 to 1953. The Cadets had been valiant in fighting through the fog of war, but back on campus it was as if a black cloud would never lift. The 1950s were rolling along with little fanfare for the Aggies.

Someone needed to stir things up. Some larger-than-life figure had to rekindle the Aggie spirit. That someone arrived in the form of a striking six foot three football coach for the ages.

Paul "Bear" Bryant may have spent only four seasons at Texas A&M, but his coaching legend still evokes passion and endless conversation at a school where football is a watercooler topic all the year long.

Caging the Bear

Paul "Bear" Bryant

When Ray George resigned as the head football coach at A&M after another dismal season in 1953 (George won just 12 games in three seasons at the helm), the athletic council and athletic director Barlow "Bones" Irvin were charged with finding a dynamic, charismatic coach for a struggling football program. But because Texas A&M was hardly a Notre Dame or Nebraska, finding—much less actually hiring—a coach with such credentials seemed a futile task. Finally, Jack Finney, a 36-year-old member of the board of directors, became exasperated. In his opinion, the names presented to the board for approval were marginal at best.

"What we were getting didn't seem to be what we were wanting," said Finney (class of '38), the youngest Aggie ever appointed to the board of directors (later board of regents). To move things forward, Finney called for the board to assemble a three-man committee that would handle the search and make their recommendation for a coaching candidate to Irvin.

The committee came up with some strong sugges-

The Memorial Student Center, shown here in 1955, has become the hub of student activity on campus. The MSC stands as a memorial to those Aggies who have lost their lives in combat.

tions, including Frank Leahy, the well-known coach of Notre Dame. And while young up-and-comers like Darrell Royal and Tom Landry were interested in the job, the man Finney wanted was Paul Bryant.

Fortunately for Finney, Bryant happened to be butting heads with the administration at the University of Kentucky, where the former Alabama letterman had been the head football coach for eight years. Better still, the fiery coach had been a huge success in the Bluegrass State, posting a 60–23–5 record and winning the only Southeastern Conference title in school history.

But at Kentucky, legendary basketball coach Adolph Rupp blew the lead whistle, much to Bryant's displeasure. Rupp won national titles in a state where basketball was king. Football—even Bryant-style—was an autumn afterthought, an athletic diversion before hoop drills tipped off in mid-October.

In January 1954, Bones Irvin told Finney that he had, in fact, talked to Bryant about the A&M job while attending the national coaches convention held that month. So Finney decided to follow up and call Bryant himself. (Bryant would later tell Finney that he had never been approached by Irvin about the A&M opening.) Aware of Bryant's displeasure with all the attention given to basketball at Kentucky, Finney told Bryant that A&M would offer him the titles of both athletic director and head football coach. "Bryant didn't like to be second in anything," Finney noted.

Finney was right: Bryant, looking for the opportunity to run a program his way, took the bait. He and Finney arranged to meet at the Baker Hotel in Dallas on a Saturday night in late January.

Did You Know?

Paul "Bear" Bryant did indeed earn his nickname from a confrontation with a circus bear in Fordyce, Arkansas, but the claim that he wrestled the bear is false. Instead, sportswriter Blackie Sherrod of *The Dallas Morning News* records that a 14-year-old Bryant was egged on by schoolyard friends to wrestle the bear for a dollar a minute. Bryant started the match, but the bear's muzzle came loose and Bryant ran for safety without collecting a dime. The nickname, on the other hand, never let go.

Junction, Texas, was home to the most infamous college football training camp in the sport's history. In 1954, the Aggies practiced on dusty, hardened fields under an unrelenting summer sun.

Once the subject of money came up at the meeting on that cold winter evening, Finney worried that the Aggies couldn't afford the aspiring and determined Bryant. But the coach badly wanted to get out of Kentucky, even if he had seen the A&M campus only once—when his Wildcats beat the Aggies 10–7 at Kyle Field in 1952.

Bryant, with his deep, gravelly voice, threw down his asking price: "What does your president make?"

"Fifteen thousand," Finney replied, referring to the salary of Marion T. Harrington.

"I don't want to make more than your president," Bryant responded.

And so the deal was struck. Bryant would be paid as much as the school president.

On February 8, 1954, Bryant landed at College Station's Easterwood Airport, where he was greeted by a throng of Cadets cheering his every step. He was quickly ushered to the Grove, an outdoor pavilion a block away from Kyle Field's north end zone.

Slamming his coat and tie down on the stage, Bryant starred in one of the school's most memorable yell practices, bellowing about regularly beating Texas one day—and everyone else. He had been on the A&M campus only a few hours, and already the idling spirit of Aggieland had cranked into overdrive.

The war years and the down times were over. The Bear was here, and it was time to play some football.

Joining Together in Junction

Bryant and his coaching staff—many of whom followed him from Kentucky—went through spring practice in 1954 and soon found that the coaching films hadn't lied: Texas A&M lacked talent and, more important to Bryant, toughness. While the spring practices were brutally physical, lasting late into the night, Bryant's most famous set of practices was about to unfold a few months later in a featureless town on the edge of the Texas Hill Country.

The ranching town of Junction, located a couple of hours west of Austin and four hours from College Station, was chosen by assistant coach Willie Zapalac, a former Aggie football player. Zapalac suggested the site because A&M had used the location for military training and educational purposes.

When 115 football players reported to College Station for fall drills in late August, Bryant told the players to start packing: Bring a pillow, blanket, and several changes of clothes. In short order, like a Corps outfit headed to basic training, the players rolled out of College Station and into football lore. As Gene Stallings, a sophomore end, would recall, the Aggies headed out in two buses . . . and came back in one.

In Junction for a relentless 10-day training session, Bryant pushed this bunch of Aggies to the brink of exhaustion and exasperation. Though he subjected the group to intense workouts in searing heat, Bryant—like most coaches in that era—wouldn't allow water breaks. Ruling with an iron fist over the burr-filled goat pasture masked as a practice field, Bryant drove many players beyond endurance. After linebacker Bill Schroeder suffered serious heatstroke on September 6, 1954, he was even kicked by the coach as he lay nearly motionless on the ground surrounded by rusty Quonset huts. Men quit the camp nightly, deserting the barracks as soon as the lights went out.

While only 35 of 115 players would survive the end of a pitiless camp in Junction and return to College Station to start the 1954 season, Bryant would describe the never-ending criticism about the session as overblown. Even Charley Moran had taken his Aggies to La Porte for a similar boot camp–style training regimen, way back in 1911.

Decades later, players who made it through the 1954 Junction grind beam with pride, claiming the camp was more than just the birth of a future championship team: It was also a bonding experience that would set many of them on the road to great success, not only in athletics but in the world of business.

Bear Bryant turned a 1–9 A&M team in 1954 into a 9–0–1 SWC champion in 1956. His 1957 team reached No. 1 in the polls before losing its last three games, and Bryant left A&M for his alma mater, Alabama, after the season ended.

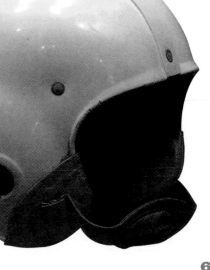

From Junction to Jubilation

Even with the much anticipated arrival of Bryant, the reclamation project for football glory at Texas A&M would have to

Jack Pardee (bottom) and John David Crow (above Pardee) ham it up for the camera just before a practice session outside Kyle Field. Pardee would go on to a successful playing and coaching career in the NFL, and Crow would win the 1957 Heisman Trophy.

wait a few more seasons. Bryant's first two years—1954 and 1955—were laced with 11 defeats, including a 1–9 campaign in '54. But under Coach Bryant, the school was close to being a Southwest Conference contender. In '54, the Aggies' most lopsided loss in conference play was a 20–7 defeat at Baylor. The rest of the league games were close calls, pulled out by the perennial favorites like Rice, TCU, and Texas.

During practices, everyone could see the young talent blossoming on the squad. Only a lack of depth on the team—caused by attrition from the Junction experience—had kept A&M from winning more games.

With freshmen running backs John David Crow and Ken Hall, quarterback Roddy Osborne, lineman Charley Krueger, and halfbacks Bobby Joe Conrad and Loyd Taylor, Bryant's signing class of 1954 was overflowing with plums. By the time these players were juniors and joined a senior class of stalwarts, the Aggies were on their way to their best season since the national championship year of 1939.

Even in 1955, with the Aggies still too young and a year away from flashing their championship mettle, A&M pounded teams like LSU and Nebraska, outscoring the two powers by a combined score of 55–0.

In the summer of 1956, all the pieces were in place for the Aggies to make a run for the SWC championship, just as Bryant had predicted. But along with the promise came a problem: Bryant had an insatiable appetite for doing everything to excess—drinking, gambling, and recruiting.

Those vices, combined with his yearning to take A&M to the top as quickly as possible (and beef up his coaching credentials in the process) proved very costly for the Aggies. The NCAA and SWC placed A&M on probation for the 1955–56 seasons after Bryant's illegal enticements in recruiting, including cash payments, were discovered.

"He was totally driven," says Dennis Goehring, a junior offensive guard and nose tackle in '56. "In his mind, the only way to get out of this hellhole was to win. And he would do it at all costs."

By 1956, the SWC lifted its probation of the Aggies. But the NCAA refused to cut short its probation, thus banning A&M from a bowl game at season's end. The sanctions didn't seem to affect the hard-nosed bunch of Bryant followers. At this football-starved college,

The Heisman Winner

John David Crow rushed for only 562 yards in 1957, but he played for one of the nation's top teams and for one of the nation's most feared coaches—Paul "Bear" Bryant. And while he was a very talented and bruising running back, and an equally adept linebacker, even Crow admits there's only one reason he won the 1957 Heisman Trophy, honoring the nation's most outstanding college football player. Bear Bryant issued an ultimatum to the media when he said, "If they don't give the Heisman Trophy to John Crow, they should stop handing out the award."

Crow remains Texas A&M's lone Heisman Trophy award winner, and his impact on the football program is a lasting one. Yet it is his service to the entire athletic department that Crow is most proud of.

"To me, the pinnacle of my success was being the athletic director at Texas A&M," said Crow, who led the department from 1988 to 1993 before taking over as a development and fund-raising figure for football. "How can a person explain his love for his father, mother, or children? If I could explain that, I could explain my love for Texas A&M."

it was all about winning games and giving A&M students and former students a glimmer of hope.

"By the time we were juniors, we all knew we had a hell of a ball club," Goehring added. "In the summer of '56, we said we're going to win the conference. We'd call each other and ask each other if we were in shape. We were all pushing each other."

Bryant was pushing even harder. For those players who wilted under his intense style of coaching, he had no sympathy. To those gutsy players who would stand up to him, he would offer his undying loyalty. It was the Bryant way—and if you understood it, you became one of the Bryant boys forever.

John David Crow, the tough, do-it-all halfback and linebacker from Springhill, Louisiana, was one of Bryant's boys. It helped that

Crow was an outstanding athlete who had led his high school team to the state championship in 1953. But with his relentless style of play, Crow epitomized the Aggies of this era. What John Kimbrough had meant to the 1939 Aggies, Crow meant to the '56 bunch.

Weathering the Storm

Just as the A&M veteran players had predicted in the summer, the Aggies bolted to a quick start in the 1956 season. With only a 14–14 tie to Houston as a blemish on a perfect record four games into the season, the Aggies and Texas Christian University were set for a major SWC matchup to open conference play. On a sultry October 20 at Kyle Field, the fouteenth-ranked Aggies and unbeaten and fourth-ranked TCU team—led by Heisman Trophy hopeful Jim Swink—were about to battle through a thunderstorm that boiled into hurricane-like conditions.

John David Crow, A&M's only Heisman Trophy winner, was the school's athletic director from 1988–93.

As the game began, the weather was ideal, albeit humid. The buzz around a sold-out Kyle Field (42,000) was thick, too, since TCU was looking for revenge for its only loss of the 1955 season—a 19–16 defeat at the hands of the Aggies. A&M was stalking up the college football charts, returning to a time when all was right at this football-loving outpost.

After warm-ups, the Aggies retreated to the locker room, where their coach warned them not to lose focus or concentration, no matter what the weather. "It doesn't matter whether a tornado or a hurricane or anything else comes through here. Just stay focused on doing your job," John David Crow recalls his coach saying.

"I was looking up at him and thinking the man must have just lost his mind. I had just been out there, and it sure as hell didn't seem possible that a big storm was going to blow through. But he obviously had an inside track on what was coming."

The storm came with a fury never seen at a football game in College Station, before or since. But the Aggies, like their coach, were veterans of hardship, having survived the rigors of Junction. The storm was just another obstacle to overcome in their quest for the SWC title.

The contest—later nicknamed the Hurricane Game—almost came to a standstill in the second quarter as horizontal rain and hail pelted fans and dangerous winds battered the stadium. Over 150 planes at Easterwood Airport were overturned, and the playing field became 100 yards of pig slop. "The wind was blowing so hard you

Dark storm clouds *build just outside Kyle Field during the A&M-TCU game in 1956. The storm that eventually swept through the area was so fierce that the contest was later dubbed the Hurricane Game by those who witnessed it.*

could hardly breathe," Swink told longtime *Waco Tribune-Herald* sportswriter Dave Campbell.

Once the storm retreated in the second half, TCU jumped to a 6–0 lead. The Horned Frogs threatened to extend the lead to 13–0 when A&M's Don Watson intercepted a pass in the end zone. Later taking advantage of clearing skies, the Aggies marched the length of the field for the game-winning score. Crow took a pass from Watson from seven yards out, with Loyd Taylor kicking the all-important extra point.

Did the game finally go according to plan?

"It went according to prayer," Bryant said.

The Aggies upended mighty TCU 7–6 in one of the most memorable games in A&M history, setting the stage for a championship run. Four victories later, all that remained was a game against UT in Austin—a black hole where other A&M football teams had gone to die.

The Longhorns' Streak Ends

From 1894 until 1956, A&M had never won a football game in Austin. But the 8–0–1 Aggies were cut from the Bryant cloth, determined to win an SWC championship even though no bowl game glistened on the horizon because of NCAA penalties.

While Oklahoma was in the middle of a 47-game winning streak and headed for its second consecutive national championship, the Aggies were gaining attention because they had become one of the best teams in the country by season's end.

But could A&M beat Texas in Austin for the first time ever?

"We were at a point where there was no way Texas was going to beat us," said Dennis Goehring. "We were that confident."

Still, the Aggies were banged up, with Crow nursing a broken bone in his foot and Pardee struggling with a shoulder injury. It didn't matter. A&M bowled over Texas 34–21 to finish a rare undefeated season in the Southwest Conference.

In the locker room after the game, players threw Bryant and his coaches in the shower. No bowl representatives were there to hand out invitations for a New Year's game, but the Aggies had risen from the depths of a one-win season in 1954 to a No. 5 ranking in 1956. Suddenly the Aggies and their loyal legion were able to display their pride on a national level.

The pinnacle was reached the following year, when *Life* magazine documented the 1957 season. In that amazing year, A&M soared to No. 1 in the country and John David Crow won the Heisman Trophy.

Bryant's Legacy

Bryant had turned around Aggie football, and A&M in the process. The 1956 Aggie football team proved football could be successful in College Station again. The school was moving from the war years toward a decade of change and growth that would alter its makeup forever.

Bryant would leave the school after the 1957 season for his dream job as head coach of his alma mater, Alabama. But he left a legacy at A&M that spawned more war stories—and success stories—than anyone thought imaginable.

Jack Finney, the young, aggressive member of the board of directors, still smiles today when he thinks of how the Bryant era panned out. Players like Jack Pardee, John David Crow, Dennis Goehring, and Gene Stallings simply refer to the Bear as Coach Bryant, and they all describe their time with him as the most memorable of their lives.

The success the Aggies of '56 had in their post-Bryant days tells the tale. Pardee went on to a sterling NFL career as a player and coach, leading the Washington Redskins, Houston Oilers, and Houston Cougars to unprecedented levels of glory. Crow won the Heisman in '57 and finished off an 11-year NFL career with four Pro Bowl appearances. After some stints in collegiate and pro coaching, Crow returned to his alma mater to become athletic director from 1988–93. Now retired and still living in College Station, Crow is often seen on campus, pointed out as one of the greatest football players in Aggie history.

Goehring became a prominent banker in College Station and resides in neighboring Bryan. Stallings coached A&M to the SWC title in 1967, later rose through the coaching ranks with the Dallas Cowboys, and ended his NFL career as the head coach of the Arizona Cardinals. Stallings's finest moment as a coach came when he led Bryant's Crimson Tide to the national title in 1992, 10 years after the death of the Bear.

Even though he would make his mark at A&M, Bryant and his wife, Mary Harmon, had been miserable when they first arrived on the campus in 1954. There was no glamour on this campus, no real football history for Bryant to draw on in recruiting. And there were too few social circles to satisfy Mary Harmon.

In those early days, it was obvious to just about everyone that Bryant was seeking a way out of Aggieland. But the school tugged at him. He enjoyed the spirit of Texas A&M, and he appreciated the loyalty and toughness this place fostered in its students. The 1956 season showed how all the intangibles of A&M could come together to forge a championship team.

"Once you were a Bryant boy, the loyalty was there," says Jack Pardee, who is retired and living on his ranch in Gause, Texas, just 30 minutes north of College Station. "It was kind of a fraternity. If he was really just a genuine S.O.B., you wouldn't keep coming back to someone like that. But Bryant had a following. If you went through it and were honest and worked with him, he didn't forget you. You were a part of him forever."

So much a part, in fact, that Bryant was buried with just one ring on either hand, even though his Alabama teams won six national titles under his watch. One of them was a special A&M letterman's ring, a gift from the Junction survivors—Bryant's boys to the end.

Bryant enjoyed the spirit of Texas A&M, and he appreciated the loyalty and toughness this place could foster in its students. The 1956 season showed how all the intangibles of A&M could come together to forge a championship team.

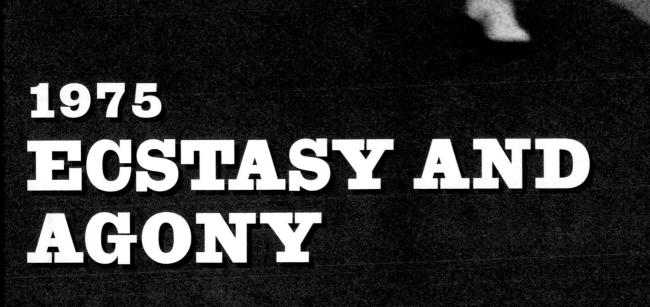

1975
ECSTASY AND
AGONY

All that was missing for the Aggies was a dominant football team. From the Bear Bryant days until 1972, A&M had secured just one Southwest Conference title.

Emory Bellard

I N THE MID-1970s, a new and improved Texas A&M began to rise up. In fact, the campus that now sprawls over 5,200 acres was in its modern infancy at the time, transforming itself into the coeducational behemoth that dominates the College Station landscape.

The vision for the university held by former board of directors chair Sterling C. Evans and school president Earl Rudder was coming into focus, and the Aggies were loving it. Of course, detractors of the school hated it: This was no cow college or military outpost anymore. Aggie jokes—told during the years when A&M's culture was as misunderstood as it was unique—no longer drew laughs in the boardrooms of the big cities.

As Texas A&M's enrollment and image were skyrocketing, the spirit of Aggieland continued to survive, and even thrive. Although there were thousands more civilian students now—with enrollment approaching 30,000 by 1975—the traditions that had shaped A&M's past held on.

The only thing missing for the Aggies was a dominant football team. From the Bear Bryant days (1954–57) until 1972, A&M had secured just one Southwest Conference title, when one of Bryant's boys, Gene Stallings, coached the Aggies to an improbable title in 1967 after beginning the year with an 0–4 record. But Stallings was unable to maintain the success.

Finally, with Texas garnering all the national attention with back-to-back national titles in 1969 and 1970, A&M officials fired Stallings after the 1971 season, when the Aggies finished with a 5–6 record—the fourth losing mark in a row.

Ironically, A&M looked toward Austin for some help. The architect of the dynamic wishbone offense, which the Longhorns had used to win 30 straight games from 1968 to 1970 under head coach Darrell Royal, was called on to lead the Aggies to prominence.

Emory Bellard, an assistant under Royal from 1967 to 1971, became A&M's new athletic director and head football coach on December 19, 1971. Bellard, known for his engaging Texas drawl and stylish pipe smoking, was about to

make a new name for himself . . . as the man who would take the struggling Aggies to the brink of a national title.

Go Get 'Em, Boys!

The New Year's Day bowl games were barely a memory when Emory Bellard called his first staff meeting on January 2, 1972. Barely knowing the names of his coaching assistants, including 27-year-old R. C. Slocum, Bellard passed around lists of the state's top recruits. Much like the recruiting demands Homer Norton had placed on his staff in 1937 (which would result in a national championship in 1939), Bellard knew A&M had to find comparable football talent to that being amassed year by year at the University of Texas.

"The whole concept of college football is to recruit," said Bellard, a former high school coach at places like Breckenridge and San Angelo Central. "You've got to get some players. We started late, and there was a great deal of anxiety on my part because our staff didn't assemble until that January 2. But I told my assistants these were the guys we were going after, and to go get them."

Before nightfall on January 3, the A&M coaching staff had talked every one of the 50 prospects on Bellard's list into visiting the A&M campus that spring. Bellard had been the former president of the Texas High School Coaches Association, and the relationships he forged ultimately led to the Aggies signing 30 outstanding prospects.

Bellard's recruits didn't let him down: The newcomers helped the

The Aggies had real success on the football field in 1967, winning the Southwest Conference title. But from 1968–71, the Aggies won just 13 games, and Emory Bellard was called on to replace Gene Stallings as head coach in 1972.

The 1974 Aggies began to turn sports fans' heads, winning eight games in a season for the first time since 1957. The following year, A&M would almost reach the pinnacle and play for its first national championship since 1939. But a 31–6 loss to Arkansas ruined a hoped-for perfect season.

Aggies win the SWC Freshman title in 1972, and 13 of the players would start on the varsity squad by the end of the fall. Players like Las Vegas's Ed Simonini, a small but quick outside linebacker, defensive back Pat Thomas, halfback Earnest "Bubba" Bean, and tight end Richard Osborne would lay the foundation for one of A&M's all-time great teams.

The season of a lifetime, however, was four years in the making. A&M struggled to a 3–8 season in Bellard's first year, since the intricacies of the option-oriented wishbone offense (two halfbacks and a fullback lined up behind the quarterback) wasn't mastered all that quickly. The 1973 season ended with a 42–13 loss to Texas to cap off a 5–6 year.

In '74, things began to change as swiftly on the football field as they were changing on the A&M campus. The Aggies were molding themselves into legitimate SWC title contenders, with a maturing offense and stingy defense. Breakthrough road victories at LSU (21–14) and Washington (28–15), and a 28–7 thrashing of Texas Tech—before a national television audience at Kyle Field—began to open some eyes, both on the national level and within the cozy confines of College Station. The Aggies had even shut out Grant Teaff's Baylor squad 20–0 on the road (Baylor's only conference loss of the season), setting the stage for a possible conference championship run.

Suddenly, A&M was 7–3 and 5–1 in the SWC heading into Austin for its traditional rivalry game with Texas. A victory would send the Aggies to the Cotton Bowl for the first time since the 1967 season. But this was Austin, and the opposing team was Texas. The combination had been a nasty one for A&M football, as the Aggies had only beaten UT three times since 1939 and only once at Memorial Stadium.

The 1974 finale against the Horns was as biting for the Aggies as the cold rain that pelted Memorial Stadium. A&M turnovers led to 14 points for Texas in the first 58 seconds of the game. Texas stung A&M 32–3 that day, sending Baylor to the Cotton Bowl as conference champions. But the calendar was about to roll over into 1975—and Texas A&M's football fortunes were about to change dramatically.

Defense Does It

Texas A&M had finished second in total defense in 1974, but the unit the Aggies rolled out in '75 was downright loaded with superstars. Simonini had been a two-time All-SWC selection and would later be named the conference's Defensive Player of the Year and earn All-America honors as a senior. Until Dat Nguyen showed up on the A&M campus in the mid-1990s, the 208-pound Simonini sat atop the all-time tackles list for an Aggie football player.

Add in Garth Ten Naple, hard-hitting middle linebacker Robert Jackson, and lockdown defensive backs like Pat Thomas and Lester Hayes, and the Aggies were filled with future NFL draft picks.

"We had a lot of mobility on defense," Coach Bellard noted. "We had a bunch of great players who were burning up wanting to get to the football."

The Aggie defense of 1975 didn't have a fashionable nickname like its Wrecking Crew predecessor, a nickname that tags the A&M defense to this day, but no one could argue with its stunning results. By the end of the '75 season, A&M was No. 1 in total defense, giving up just 175 yards a game and only six touchdowns for the year. A&M shut out two opponents (Ole Miss and Kansas State) and held four other teams to single digits in scoring.

Meanwhile, on offense, A&M was grinding down opponents with its relentless rushing attack out of the wishbone. With Bubba Bean and Skip Walker at halfback and the redwood thighs of freshman fullback George Woodard churning through defenses, the Aggies scored 33 or more points five times that season, including a 39–8 blowout of LSU at Tiger Stadium in Baton Rouge. The steady Mike Jay at quarterback, the sure-handed Richard Osborne at tight end, and the shifty Carl Roaches at split end gave A&M plenty of weaponry to make a run at the national college football championship.

Did You Know?

Legendary University of Texas coach Darrell Royal is often credited with inventing the wishbone offense that helped UT win national titles in 1969 and 1970. But it was actually Texas assistant coach Emory Bellard who drew up the scheme in the spring of 1968. Bellard took his wishbone offense to Texas A&M in 1972, taking the Aggies to unprecedented success in 1975–76, with consecutive 10-win seasons. Bellard's wishbone would be copied by many coaches, including Barry Switzer at Oklahoma and Alabama's Paul "Bear" Bryant.

The Aggie defense of 1975 didn't have a fashionable nickname like its Wrecking Crew predecessor, a nickname that tags the A&M defense to this day, but no one could argue with its stunning results.

The 1975 coaching staff
included head coach Emory
Bellard (kneeling) and a young
assistant from Orange, Texas—
R. C. Slocum (fifth from right,
standing). Bellard is retired and
living at the edge of the Texas Hill
Country, in Horseshoe Bay.
Slocum became head coach of
the Aggies in 1989.

The Aggies did just that, busting out to a 9–0 record heading into the Texas game. Not since the 1939 national championship had an A&M football team burned through a season unbeaten. To the hallelujahs of Aggies everywhere, this team was dominating on the field and scaling the college football polls.

Yet amid all the talk of an undefeated season and a shot at the national title, A&M players and fans were wary. After all, the idea of playing fifth-ranked Texas—with all of the paranoia that the one-sided series had created—wasn't cause for early celebration. Across the nation, however, things were falling into place for the Aggies. Oklahoma, which was aiming for its second straight national title, had been ranked No. 1 all season long, but it was upset by Kansas 23–3 on the same day that A&M cruised past SMU 36–3.

Oklahoma slid to sixth in the Associated Press poll, while Ohio State moved into the top spot, followed by No. 2 Nebraska and third-ranked Texas A&M. The Sooners then did A&M a huge favor, toppling the Cornhuskers to push the Aggies into the No. 2 spot. The Aggies were on the verge.

Bring on the Longhorns

Richard Osborne, the gifted tight end for the Aggies, says he knew A&M would beat Texas right after the 38–9 pummeling of Texas

Tech midway through the season. "We were invincible," he recalled.

But those sports fans who had followed the A&M football program for years weren't so sure. Even with starting Longhorn quarterback Marty Akins hobbled with a knee injury entering the game, there was just something about the Longhorns that brought out the worst—or worst luck—in the Aggie team.

In 1940, Texas stopped A&M's 19-game winning streak, keeping the Aggies from winning back-to-back national titles. In 1963, A&M had nearly pulled off one of the most memorable upsets in school history, but a controversial out-of-bounds call of an interception in the Longhorns' end zone allowed No. 1 UT to hold on to a tainted 15–13 victory. Add in the first-minute implosion of A&M against Texas in the 1974 game, and the Aggies were saddled with one notion whenever they played the Horns: Here we go again.

But this time the season seemed different. While 9–1 Texas owned the nation's top-ranked offense, A&M's defense was so stifling that even the Longhorns might have trouble moving the ball.

Surprisingly, A&M players were relaxed leading up to the game. The day before the showdown at Kyle Field, ABC cameras were shooting mug shots of the team for the Friday-after-Thanksgiving national telecast. The Aggies were hamming it up for the cameras, seemingly oblivious to the high stakes that surrounded the game of the decade for Texas A&M.

On the other hand, the fans who shoehorned into Kyle Field on a comfortable November afternoon were wound as tight as a bunch of wide-eyed freshmen in the Corps. "It was equal parts angst and confidence," said longtime A&M follower Don Jones, who watched the game amid a fire code–breaking crowd of 56,679 (9,000 more than capacity). "When you've been down and kicked, and then you have a chance to beat these guys . . . it was all about beating Texas instead of thinking about a national title."

The game started with a bang, as Emory Bellard opened up his playbook and called an end-around to Carl Roaches on the Aggies' second play from scrimmage. The play stunned both the Longhorn defense and the Aggie crowd as Roaches rocketed downfield for 47 yards.

A&M then took a 10–0 lead on a four-yard touchdown catch by Osborne. But the Texas hex struck back as Raymond Clayborn took a punt 64 yards for a touchdown to cut the lead to 10–7, which remained the score heading into the fourth quarter. By then, Texas quarterback Marty Akins had left the game after aggravating his knee injury. And big George Woodard was beginning to wear on the Longhorns,

Linebacker Ed Simonini was small in stature, but he blossomed into an All-American. Simonini was the anchor of an Aggie unit that led the nation in total defense in '75.

scoring on a one-yard touchdown run to give the Aggies a 17–10 lead.

The tension was near breaking point when A&M's Bubba Bean gave the Aggies the big play they needed to secure the win, as he burst through the line of scrimmage on a trap play and ran 73 yards to the one-inch line (replays would show Bean scored on the play). Texas forced a field goal, but A&M would never look back en route to a monumental 20–10 victory.

Fans spilled out onto the field, celebrating a historic victory in Aggieland. Second-ranked Texas A&M had beaten No. 5 Texas, the football program that had tormented the Aggies for decades.

R. C. Slocum, who has coached all but one season at A&M since 1972, said the win over Texas was an exhilarating one, but he remained leery because there was one last regular season game with Arkansas still to be played.

"The Texas game was a big, big win for us," he said. "There was just tremendous excitement. But it was just hard to come back the next day and get to work on another good team."

When quarterback Mike Jay went down with an injury in the Texas game, the Aggies lost an important ingredient in their wishbone attack.

From Celebration to Devastation

Around Aggieland in the 1970s, the school's search for regional and national exposure was an all-important task, with televised football games opening the widest window for the state of Texas and the country as a whole to see a changed Texas A&M. So when ABC officials approached Emory Bellard about moving the Aggies' game with Arkansas from its traditional early November slot to December 6—just eight days following the Texas game—Bellard could hardly decline the offer.

Bellard had been trying to build his program into a national power, and had done just that in four short years. With his 1975 Aggies owning a perfect 10–0 record and No. 2 national ranking, A&M seemed to be on a roll. Surely it was capable of handling a good Arkansas team, even in Little Rock.

But the Texas game—with all of the emotions this rivalry stirs in the Aggies—had sapped the A&M players and coaches the week before. Besides that, quarterback Mike Jay had suffered two compressed vertebrae in his back late in the Texas game, forcing backup David Shipman into service to close out what was hoped to be an undefeated season.

Ironically, Arkansas coach Frank Broyles had seen Jay go down in the Texas game, since he was a guest color commentator for ABC Sports during the A&M-Texas shootout. "When you lose your quarterback," Broyles ominously told one writer after the game, "you lose your whole offense."

Still, the Aggies were immensely confident about playing the

University of Arkansas—anywhere, and with any quarterback. After all, A&M had just beaten fifth-ranked Texas and had beaten Arkansas 20–10 the year before.

"We were going to dominate," Richard Osborne recalled. "We were going to run the ball and win the ball game. We thought we were good enough to beat them in hell. Or if hell froze over, we'd beat them on the ice."

As it turned out, hell materialized in the form of a cold, dreary day at War Memorial Stadium. There, the Aggies had to confront an 8–2 Arkansas team that had been improving with each passing week. They weren't the Aggies, especially on defense, but the Razorbacks had enough weapons to make this an interesting game.

But it didn't start out that way: The first half remained scoreless between the Aggies and Razorbacks because both teams were sloppy handling the ball. A&M's Lester Hayes recovered an Arkansas fumble at the Razorback 29-yard line, but the Aggies' scoring drive stalled at the five. Talented kicker Tony Franklin then missed a chip-shot field goal. It was a sign of bad things to come.

Then, just before halftime, Arkansas caught a major break—catching a prayer of a touchdown pass—with 34 seconds left in the second quarter. At the A&M 41-yard line, Arkansas quarterback Scott Bull threw toward the end zone, where a double team of Aggie defenders waited. But the ball somehow sailed past A&M's Lester Hayes and Jackie Williams to five foot nine receiver Teddy Barnes, who hauled in one of the most remarkable touchdown catches in Arkansas history. The catch was so memorable that a huge picture of it hangs in Arkansas's posh athletic offices even today.

"The catch we made in the end zone was the luckiest thing I ever saw," said Arkansas assistant Jesse Branch. "It stuck in his face mask."

The Aggies were down just 7–0 at halftime, but the deficit might as well have been three touchdowns. Arkansas was confident and giddy, the Aggies edgy and uncomfortable. The national title contender from College Station was vulnerable and—for the first time that season—beatable.

The score would mushroom to 24–0 in Arkansas's favor when David Shipman was popped, forcing him to fumble in his own end zone. When the final whistle blew, the Aggies' dream of a national championship season had dissipated into the cold, drizzly air. Arkansas beat A&M 31–6 in a game that was moved for television.

To this day, coaches and players from both sides agree that had the game stayed with its November 1 scheduled date, the Aggies likely would have beaten Arkansas and had their perfect season.

As the Aggies slowly boarded buses to the Little Rock Airport, R. C. Slocum recalls how miserable he felt after the chance of a lifetime had evaporated. On the charter plane back to College Station, a Cotton

Did You Know?

As Bubba Bean and the rest of the Aggies celebrated the huge 20–10 win over Texas in 1975 to run Texas A&M's record to 10–0, the Aggie running back was focused on keeping this dream season alive.

Then the *Sports Illustrated* jinx hit. Bean adorned the cover of the national sports magazine with the headline, "Texas A&M Stakes Its Claim: Bubba Bean Shreds Texas."

Just eight days after beating Texas, the banged-up Aggies fell to the Arkansas Razorbacks 31–6 in one of the most disappointing losses in A&M football history. The loss kicked the Aggies out of their first national championship race since the 1939 season.

But for Bean, the cover shot on *Sports Illustrated* didn't fade away in the memories of Aggie fans everywhere. In fact, Bean says he receives countless requests for autographs on the magazine, usually right before football season.

"Coming from the country and not having been exposed to that kind of stuff, it really didn't mean that much to me," said Bean, who owns his own construction company in Bryan–College Station. "I didn't know it was such an honor or a privilege to be on the cover of *Sports Illustrated*. I had seen the magazine, but I didn't know it would have the impact it's had over the years."

Other Aggies have been on the coveted *SI* cover in football action photos, (John David Crow made it as a St. Louis Cardinal) but none had been the focal point of the cover like Bean.

A copy of that 1975 *Sports Illustrated* hangs on a wall inside the Texas A&M Sports Museum.

"Over the years, I've realized that was a special situation, and I feel honored that I was recognized that week," Bean added. "Unfortunately, the season didn't turn out the way we wanted it to, but it's still special."

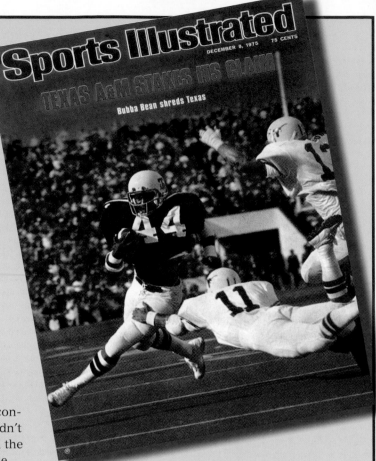

Bowl Express sign on the bulkhead was ripped down by players in frustration. A&M football had reached a new low, but not because of probation or a one-win season. This was the agony of defeat in its purest form, since the reality of a perfect season had seemed so within reach just a week before.

"That hurt, and it hurt bad," Bellard recalled 27 years later. "But it's like most things . . . if you're going to have a hurt, you have to get to the point where you have great expectations. There was a point in A&M football when there weren't many high expectations."

The Loss's Ripple Effect

After finishing the regular season 10–1, losing to Arkansas in the televised finale, the Aggies missed out on the Cotton Bowl and a national title tilt with Georgia. Instead, A&M accepted a Liberty Bowl bid to play the University of Southern California.

A dispirited Aggie squad fell apart and ended the season with a 20–0 thumping at the hands of USC. To add to the pain of losing its last two games and dropping to eleventh in the polls, A&M would watch No. 1 Ohio State fall to UCLA 23–10 in the Rose Bowl, theoretically opening the door for a possible A&M national title had the Aggies made it to the Cotton Bowl. Instead, Oklahoma would beat Michigan 14–6 in the Orange Bowl to claim a second straight national crown.

On the A&M campus, the hangover from Little Rock lasted for weeks, if not years. In fact, if you bring up the score 31–6 at an Aggie cocktail party today, the long faces automatically tell the time and place.

Richard Osborne, the Aggies' fiery tight end, says he will never get over that day in Arkansas. R. C. Slocum maintains that the loss kept the A&M program from catapulting to a new level in college football. Back-to-back national titles, he claims, might have been a possibility with the number of players who returned to the team in 1976 (a 10–2 season).

"It would have changed the whole course of A&M football history," Slocum says. "If you ask me the most significant game in the last [three decades] of A&M's history, that game was it because we could have won the national championship. Games like the Arkansas game are indelibly marked on you. You've got scars that will be with you a lifetime."

As for Bellard, the classy coach perhaps never recovered professionally from the collapse of the 1975 season, ultimately resigning under fire four games into the 1978 season. Yet Bellard accomplished much during his six-plus years as head coach. He had brought A&M from the depths to rare heights, capped by the 10–0 run in '75. What's more, attendance soared during his tenure, as Kyle Field began to build its national reputation as one of the nation's most intimidating stadiums. Crowds had doubled in size to over 50,000, and donations to the Aggie Club (now the 12th Man Foundation) were increasing tenfold. Plans for the 1980 stadium expansion (which took Kyle Field to over 72,000 seats) were drawn up during Bellard's watch, and suites on the stadium's west side sold out in one day when they went on sale, as a delighted Bellard looked on.

"I'm very proud," Bellard says of taking A&M to a new stratosphere in football. "That's what I went there to do."

Thanks to Bellard, the days of feeling inferior to Texas—or any other school, for that matter—were as distant as the old male and military ways of a half century ago. No longer just a spirited bystander, Texas A&M University had become a major player on all fronts.

"What Emory Bellard did was change the perception of Texas A&M," says Aggie Don Jones. "Even after the Arkansas loss, there was a feeling that we will never be where we were again."

R. C. Slocum *calls the Arkansas game the most significant in the past 30 years.*

Coach Jackie Sherrill takes a ride on his players' shoulders following a big win over Arkansas in 1983.

1985
THOSE COTTON-PICKIN' AGGIES

A&M officials were determined to spark a fire for their football program. As it turned out, the spark exploded into a full-fledged bonfire, as controversy and success walked hand in hand through a tumultuous and tantalizing seven years of football from 1982 to 1988.

Jackie Sherrill

I N THE EARLY 1980s, those who could light the biggest cigars and slap the most backs were the kingpins of college football. Bowl games were run like beauty pageants, with only the most glamorous and glitzy teams walking down the runway with postseason invitations.

In fact, on college campuses, overzealous football boosters packed as much punch as any university president did. Just ask SMU, whose subsequent NCAA probations for recruiting violations were only the first in a string of scandals involving Southwest Conference teams during the decade.

At Texas A&M, backroom moving and shaking was as much a part of the landscape as Cadet khaki and Midnight Yell Practice. But the Aggies were in a definite slump. Emory Bellard had abruptly resigned after the fourth game of the 1978 season. The next coach, Tom Wilson, hadn't been able to propel the team to greatness. In his three-plus seasons, A&M went 21–19.

The slump only made A&M officials more determined to spark a fire for their football program. As it turned out, the spark exploded into a full-fledged bonfire, as controversy and success walked hand in hand through a tumultuous and tantalizing seven years of football from 1982 to 1988.

A Pivotal Hire

H. R. "Bum" Bright was the chairman of the board of regents in 1981, when A&M set in motion one of the most talked-about coaching hires in college football. After firing Wilson following the '81 season—in which the 7–4 Aggies nevertheless won the Independence Bowl—Bright, a rich and powerful oilman from Dallas, decided to get some advice from the old guard in college football. He contacted four football icons: Oklahoma's Bud Wilkinson, Texas's Darrell Royal, Dallas Cowboys scouting guru Gil Brandt, and another familiar name around Aggieland—Alabama's Paul "Bear" Bryant.

Florida State coach Bobby Bowden and former Michigan coach Bo Schembechler were candidates for the A&M position in 1982. Schembechler looked closely at the opportunity before ultimately staying put at Michigan.

Each of the four men was asked to draw up a list of his top five coaches in college football and submit them to Bright. "I took the 20 names on the list," said Bright, "and the No. 1–rated guy was Bo Schembechler. The No. 2 guy was Bobby Bowden, and Jackie Sherrill was ranked fourth."

Schembechler had built Michigan into a national power and frequent Rose Bowl participant, while Bowden was transforming Florida State into a football giant that would dominate the next 20 years of college play. Sherrill, meanwhile, was a brash young coach who had led Pittsburgh to three straight 11–1 seasons from 1979–81. With hotshot quarterback Dan Marino set to return to Pitt in 1982, Sherrill's Panthers were considered a preseason favorite for the national title.

At first, Schembechler seemed the leading candidate for the Aggie coaching job, since the Michigan man had family ties in Louisiana. But he had just recuperated from a heart attack and wanted a 10-year guaranteed contract. Bright wanted his coach around long-term, at least healthwise, but he was hesitant to offer that big a package.

Bowden declined any offer. So Bright decided to go after Jackie Sherrill, who had coached with Bryant at Alabama and had the Bear's highest endorsement.

Bright sent A&M regents William McKenzie and John Blocker to Pittsburgh to interview Sherrill. They were persuasive enough to get the coach to fly to College Station for a visit. Once there, Sherrill met

Jackie Sherrill created the 12th Man Kickoff Team in 1983, hoping to capitalize on the energy and enthusiasm of the A&M student body. The team was made up of non-scholarship walk-ons.

with school president Dr. Frank Vandiver. It didn't take long for Vandiver to take a liking to the 38-year-old coach and to sense that this was the man to rouse the A&M football program from its slumber.

Sherrill was not going to come cheaply, but that was just fine with an A&M administration determined to lift the Aggie football program out of middle-of-the-pack football. The regents hired Sherrill on January 20, 1982, awarding him a six-year contract worth $282,000 annually. Sherrill was also named athletic director, and his deal included television and radio show fees, a car, and a housing allowance. Back then, a contract that size was shocking to the college football world, prompting *Sports Illustrated* to write a scathing commentary about the new deal.

In hindsight, the hiring of Sherrill—even with the controversy over his new contract—showed incredible vision on the part of the A&M athletic program. This was a cutting-edge move at a time when college football was in the throes of changing from a regional sport to something approaching big business.

As courageous as it had been, Sherrill's hire brought still more disdain—this time from A&M fans—when the Aggies did not start winning overnight. It would take three years of slow progress before A&M began to rise from the depths of mediocrity. But the goose-bump season of 1985 was on its way, and the spirit of Aggieland was about to star on the national stage.

Momentum in '84

In Jackie Sherrill's first 31 games as Texas A&M's head coach, the Aggies won just 14 times. In 1984, after coming off an embarrassing 28–0 shellacking at Arkansas, A&M football appeared to be headed nowhere—as did Sherrill's tenure as head coach.

With games against ranked opponents TCU and Texas still ahead

Sounding Off

"When we were looking for a coach, we were kind of at a crossroads. We were either going to just continue trying to field a winning team or we were going to actually get there. I liked Jackie Sherrill and his great attitude from the start. And the board was all for his hefty contract, looking on it as a corporate decision for the future. Like them, I thought, If we get the right man, let's keep him. I thought we'd come out all right, and we did."

—Dr. Frank Vandiver, A&M president 1981–88

to close out the '84 schedule, it seemed as if A&M's gamble on the slick-ster from Pittsburgh would end in failure.

It was an unexpected locker-room rant that turned things around. Just before a practice leading up to the TCU game, All-America defen-sive end Ray Childress—normally a quiet type, though an assassin on the field—tore into his teammates. He stood up and heatedly demanded a change of fortune in the football program. It may have been a tantrum, but it was also a speech that, to this day, many observers claim was one of the most poignant and heartfelt in A&M foot-ball history.

"He screamed, 'I am not—and we are not—going to lose this game!,' " Sherrill recalls. "It was unreal. He was determined not to let a losing season happen, and it didn't. Childress turned the program around."

That day, Childress took the lead and played perhaps his most dominating game as a collegiate, despite being double- and triple-teamed on almost every play. The 8–2 Horned Frogs—who could have nailed down a Cotton Bowl berth with a win—were stunned at Kyle Field as A&M rolled to a 35–21 victory, setting up a showdown with No. 13–ranked Texas.

The Aggies hadn't defeated Texas since 1980, having been swatted away in 1983 by the Longhorns 45–13. But because A&M had beaten up on TCU just a week before, the Aggies actually felt confident as they walked into Austin's Memorial Stadium on a cool and clear Saturday night in early December.

The swagger turned to dancing when the 5–5 Aggies shocked the sellout crowd with a 20–0 onslaught of the 7–2–1 Horns in the first half. In the second half, some early UT momentum lost steam after a blocked field goal return by Aggie defensive lineman Scott Polk—one of the most memorable plays in the Aggie-Longhorn series. That play set up an A&M field goal in the third quarter, and A&M would stake a 23–0 lead. The Aggies would never be threatened the rest of the game, and went on to blow out the Horns 37–12.

The majority of the squad would be returning in 1985—including highly touted quarterback Kevin Murray, who missed the '84 campaign because of a broken ankle. Feeding off that happy set of circumstances and the frenzy that followed the toppling of two ranked teams in con-secutive weeks, Aggies everywhere were counting the days until the '85 season opener.

Kevin Murray became one of A&M's most dynamic quarterbacks, leading the Aggies to two SWC titles.

Kevin's Comeback

Late in the 1983 season and in early 1984, Texas A&M quar-terback Kevin Murray was beginning to look like one of the

Johnny Holland helped A&M continue its tradition of producing top-flight linebackers.

nation's most promising run/pass threats. Blessed with quick feet and a rocket arm, Murray was to give the Aggies a rare weapon at the most important position on the field.

Still, A&M's offense had been anemic in 1983 and 1984, with Murray's talents shackled by the inexperienced cast of players around him. Sherrill's offensive coaching staff had emphasized a power running game, drawing on the strengths of running backs Roger Vick and Anthony Toney. Future tight-end star Rod Bernstine also saw time as a running back before moving over to his signature position in 1985.

Sherrill decided to make changes in his offensive coaching staff, hiring Vanderbilt offensive coordinator Lynn Amedee to install a sophisticated, balanced attack that could take advantage of Murray's many talents.

"Jackie showed us films of Vanderbilt, and Vanderbilt was in Tuscaloosa tearing up Alabama," Murray said. "Then Vanderbilt was tearing up Florida in Gainesville. I was thinking, 'Damn, we're going to be running this offense?' That was exciting."

The Aggies had their shot at Alabama in the first game of the 1985 season, but with Murray's ankle still not 100 percent healthy, A&M couldn't move the ball consistently, eventually falling to the Crimson Tide 23–10. Yet through three quarters, the underdog Aggies were tied 10–10 with mighty Alabama before a tough crowd at Birmingham's Legion Field. Murray may have limped through the game (he threw off of one foot for most of the contest), but the Aggies still proved their play had risen far and above that of the mediocre 1982–84 seasons.

"We went in there as the underdogs and lost the game, but I think that game actually gave us some confidence," said Johnny Holland, one of A&M's all-time greats at inside linebacker. "And we just rolled from there."

Well, not exactly. The Aggies cruised past Northeast Louisiana and Tulsa, but they barely escaped Texas Tech, when the Aggie defense batted away a two-point conversion attempt with less than a minute to play to preserve a 28–27 victory. That was followed by a 43–16 demolition of the University of Houston, which meant that A&M carried a 4–1 record into Waco for a matchup with Southwest Conference contender Baylor. But another disappointment was waiting: Before a sellout crowd at Baylor Stadium, Murray played his poorest game of the year and was replaced by backup Craig Stump in the second half. The Bears scored the game-winning touchdown on a fourth-down play from the one-yard line in the fourth quarter to notch a 20–15 victory.

Despite the 4–2 record, by mid-season the Aggies and Murray had found the cohesion they needed for a championship. Murray's ankle (which had been shattered in an ugly fall against Arkansas State in 1984) had healed, and both sides of the team were playing top-notch football. The Aggies were averaging over 200 yards per game in rushing and passing, while the defense did not give up more than 17 points per game over the final five games of the season.

An unranked A&M team had begun the season with hopes of just making it to a bowl game. By November, the Aggies were in the top 20 rankings, their first appearance there since the 1978 team finished nineteenth in the Associated Press final poll.

Still, A&M needed help to win a conference championship. And there were plenty of obstacles to overcome—specifically, a daunting November stretch run that featured perennial conference contenders SMU, Arkansas, and Texas.

On the bright side, all three of those teams were scheduled to come to Kyle Field. And also coming to the home stadium was a new and growing all-sports network called ESPN. What transpired over the next 26 days would go down in A&M football history as perhaps the most dramatic and spine-tingling gamut of games in over a century of Aggie football.

A November to Remember

As ESPN began its first season of expanded coverage of college football, the network was searching for a new angle to capture viewers. College football fans were accustomed to watching the game of the week on ABC, the longtime network of the sport. ESPN was looking for a southern school that would be receptive to broadcasting night games in the coldest month of the season—a school with spirit and unusual story lines, and, even better, an underdog making a run at a conference title. It was also hoping for coverage of a nationally known coach, exciting players, and colorful matchups on the field.

What ESPN found was Texas A&M. In a rare TV occurrence, ESPN signed on to televise in prime time A&M's final three home games. In today's jumble of televised games and conference TV pacts, no one team could ever garner so much valuable airtime in such a tight timespan. But back then, A&M turned out to be the perfect showcase for the network's prime-time games. And Jackie Sherrill and his fired-up team took full advantage of this out-of-the-blue publicity.

"The whole country got a good look at the Band, the students, the atmosphere, some of the academic programs, and the Bonfire on national TV," Sherrill noted. "The only ones who really knew about those things before were the Aggies themselves."

It was a deal made in heaven: ESPN used the Aggies to build its Saturday night ratings, while the Aggies used ESPN to spread the word

"The whole country got a good look at the Band, the students, the atmosphere, some of the academic programs, and the Bonfire on national TV," Sherrill noted. "The only ones who really knew about those things before were the Aggies themselves."

Murray is second on the all-time list for passing yards at A&M with 6,506 over four seasons.

to everyone watching that A&M football was a force to be reckoned with.

Against SMU on a cold and misty night at Kyle Field, the Aggies used a wet field to neutralize the Mustangs' salty option game. But the going was still tough. Kevin Murray was struggling with a rib injury and could barely throw the ball 20 yards. After an eight-play, 91-yard touchdown drive by the Ponies to take a 17–16 lead with 4:46 left in the game, the Aggies needed some seriously big plays to keep a dream season alive.

Things were looking good after big runs by tailback Roger Vick and pass receptions by third-down specialist Keith Woodside pushed the ball into SMU territory with less than two minutes remaining. But at the SMU 30-yard line, the Aggies' surge stalled. It was time to bring in the kicker.

Tony Franklin, A&M's barefoot, all-world kicker from 1975–78, had set the standard for placekicking in an Aggie uniform. So it seemed fitting that on this tense night at Kyle Field, with all the pressure of a nationally televised game, Tony's brother, Eric, kicked his way into Aggie football lore. With 1:48 left, Eric Franklin booted a 47-yard field goal that seemed to flutter in the wind like a kite at the beach. The ball came down just over the crossbar to give the Aggies the crucial and heart-pounding victory, 19–17.

Said Sherrill, in his ever confident manner: "I didn't send Eric Franklin out there to miss."

Setting Up a Showdown

Having chalked up a 6–2 record plus a defeat of SMU, the Aggies still had their work cut out for them before a Thanksgiving night showdown with Texas. They not only had to beat Arkansas and TCU but they needed a Baylor loss sometime before the end of November. The Bears were tied with the Aggies and Longhorns in the SWC race, with one loss apiece, but they owned any tiebreaker over A&M by virtue of their 20–15 victory over the Aggies earlier in the season.

A&M did its part, beating Arkansas in a tight 10–6 game—again on ESPN on another cool, damp night at Kyle Field. And while they were busy giving TCU a 53–6 pounding in Fort Worth, the Aggies found out the best news possible—that Texas had upset Baylor in a 17–10 thriller.

The unthinkable was about to happen: Texas A&M and Texas—

both ranked teams with one SWC loss each—were to play in College Station for the right to go to the Cotton Bowl as conference champions.

A&M hadn't won a conference title since 1967, when quarterback Edd Hargett led the team to the Cotton Bowl (the SWC's anchor bowl since 1936). For the Aggies, it had been a long 18 years of near misses, coaching turnover, and suffering.

Finally, though, the dream was here: No. 15–ranked A&M and No. 18–ranked Texas were going to play in a winner-take-all matchup on ESPN.

"It was unbelievable," recalled Kevin Murray. "It was a miracle season. All I can remember is that the students and the alums were so joyous because they could feel us coming together. Everybody had the same purpose and the same goals."

As Thanksgiving Day dawned, the chills down the spine had less to do with the cold November air than with the scintillating feeling around the Texas A&M campus. Fans and media descended upon College Station in hordes, filling up the campus 10 hours before game

Fans and media descended on College Station in hordes, filling up the campus 10 hours before game time.

Wide receiver Jeff Nelson hauls in another pass from Kevin Murray. The Aggies scored 35 second-half points to roll past the Longhorns and claim their first outright SWC championship since 1967.

Sounding Off

"I remember coming out of the locker room and feeling the stadium shaking. The 12th Man towels were everywhere. I think the 12th Man tradition really hit home that night, and I understood what it really meant. I think the fans that year—and every year—at Texas A&M played a big part in our football team. But that year, they were really outstanding."

—Johnny Holland, A&M linebacker (1983–86) and former Green Bay Packers standout

time. Local radio stations blared the "Aggie War Hymn" every hour on the hour. If you were a college football fan—and an Aggie as well—November 28, 1985 was a red-letter day in your life.

When kickoff approached, a then record crowd of 77,607 crammed Kyle Field. Fans cheered the punters in warm-ups as if they were rock stars, and by the time Texas A&M's players rolled out of the tunnel, the scene was as intimidating as it was mesmerizing. The 12th Man towel tradition—towels waved in support of A&M's 12th Man Kickoff Team of 11 walk-ons—had overtaken the stadium.

The Loudest Night in Kyle Field History

Once the game kicked off between the Aggies and Longhorns on that chilly November night, the electricity in the stands remained palpable even after both teams failed to score many points in the first half. The Aggies led just 7–0 at halftime after Murray hit receiver Jeff Nelson for a 10-yard touchdown pass early in the second quarter.

But in the third quarter, Murray and the Aggies put on an offensive show that sent the already rocking stadium into a frenzy. The Aggies scored 21 points in a flurry of touchdown passes from Murray, while the Aggie defense was about to finish their eleventh straight quarter without allowing a touchdown.

With the Aggies sensing the kill, Texas made a fatal mistake on offense. The Longhorns tried to wait out the storm—or more specifically the *roar*—cascading down the three decks of Kyle Field. Backed up inside his own 20-yard line and facing a passing situation, UT quarterback Bret Stafford (who had replaced starter Todd Dodge) refused to snap the ball until the din subsided. With each passing minute of delay, Stafford looked to the referee for help. There was none.

"It was the worst thing he could have done," said Murray, recalling each play of the contest 17 years later. "Obviously, he had never been in that environment. He could have taken the crowd out of it by making a play or two. He committed suicide by waiting to snap the ball."

For what seemed like five minutes, Stafford and the Horns were completely overwhelmed by the howls that filled the stadium. It was the defining moment in the game, and it helped change the momentum of the A&M-Texas series. A&M would go on to win nine of its next 10 games against its chief rival.

Texas finally snapped the ball, and A&M defenders swarmed in for the quarterback sack. Suddenly, amid pure bedlam, this long-

Linebacker John Roper (83) bears down on Texas quarterback Bret Stafford, as running back Roger Vick (43) strolls in for a touchdown. The Aggies' 42–10 win remains the largest margin of victory for Texas A&M in the history of the Texas series.

awaited game was over—and the fourth quarter hadn't even started. The Aggies would add 14 points to their lead in the final quarter and cap off a dream season with a 42–10 victory over Texas. It remains the largest margin of victory for A&M over Texas in school history.

And it all happened on ESPN, on Thanksgiving night at home, and on Jackie Sherrill's forty-second birthday. After the game, wild celebrations engulfed College Station, as revelers closed off three lanes of traffic in the Northgate bar district. Impromptu yell practices took place as wannabe Yell Leaders scaled the roof of the Dixie Chicken to lead the roaring crowd.

Who could blame the Aggies? Texas A&M was headed to its first Cotton Bowl in 18 years, beating its nemesis Texas in such style that the game remains a topic of conversation around Aggie Thanksgiving tables to this day.

The Train's Still Rolling

The Aggies would go on to whip Auburn in the Cotton Bowl on New Year's Day of 1986, stopping Heisman Trophy winner Bo Jackson on four memorable downs inside the 10-yard line to preserve the 36–16 victory. The win catapulted A&M to a final ranking of No. 6 in the Associated Press poll, the Aggies' highest season-ending ranking since the 1956 crew finished fifth overall. No A&M team has finished higher in the final polls since.

93

Alex Morris jumps all over Longhorn quarterback Bret Stafford, who had to battle unending noise from the Kyle Field crowd and the suffocating play of a supercharged Aggie defense.

Jackie Sherrill *enjoys the celebrations inside the locker room following the 1986 Cotton Bowl victory over Auburn.*

Did You Know?

When Texas A&M stopped Auburn Heisman Trophy winner Bo Jackson four times inside the A&M 10-yard line to seal a 36–16 victory in the 1986 Cotton Bowl, it marked the start of a string of successes against the nation's most outstanding football players. In the 1988 Cotton Bowl, A&M beat Heisman winner Tim Brown's Notre Dame squad 35–10, and followed that up with a 65–14 thrashing of Heisman Trophy winner Ty Detmer and his BYU team in the 1990 Holiday Bowl.

Because the Aggies won six straight games to finish off 1985 with a 10–2 record, many players on the squad believe they could have played Miami or Oklahoma for the national championship and won: A&M was that hot by season's end.

The Sooners eventually took the national title with an 11–1 record, but the impact of the 1985 season on A&M football would be felt for the next two decades. Jackie Sherrill had instilled a new winning attitude in Aggie football, and that feeling would translate into two more SWC titles in 1986 and 1987.

But those fantastic seasons would soon be tinged with sadness, when Sherrill left A&M under fire in 1988. His program had been targeted for recruiting violations that included an alleged fund of hush money to keep players from squawking about improprieties in the program to the NCAA and the media. Ultimately, school president William H. Mobley forced Sherrill out in December of '88 and appointed defensive coordinator R. C. Slocum head coach. John David Crow, the school's 1957 Heisman Trophy winner, took over as athletic director.

Sherrill's tenure at A&M had wrought a maroon-and-white miracle. He had taken the Aggie football program to new heights and given the loyal A&M fans a stage for strutting their unrivaled spirit. To this day, Sherrill—now the head coach at Mississippi State—considers his stint at A&M a gratifying one. In fact, mention players like Kevin

Auburn Heisman Trophy winner Bo Jackson was stopped four times inside the 10-yard line by the Aggie defense in the second half of the 1986 Cotton Bowl. Texas A&M went on to beat the Tigers 36–16 to cap a magical 10–2 season.

The 12th Man Kickoff Team

Jackie Sherrill stood on the second stack of Aggie Bonfire in the fall of 1982. Jerry Jeff Walker's Texana music was piped in from the perimeter of Duncan Field, the Bonfire site that spreads out just beyond the manicured front lawn of the school president. Bright-eyed, saw-dust-covered students handed him pliers and offered instructions on how to wire the thick logs to one another on what would be a tower-ing 55-foot stack.

"If these kids are this tough and this crazy, and give so much back to their school," Sherrill thought, "then I can find 10 to go down the field on my kickoff team."

And so the idea for the famed 12th Man Kickoff Team was born. The kickoff team was made up of walk-ons—students culled from the legions of passionate fans. This would be the hook Sherrill needed to spark his young but still floundering football team.

An Overwhelming Response

Determined to bring his ideas to fruition, Sherrill made his first stop at Duncan Dining Hall, where he thought he could rustle up 12 guys (10 starters and two reserves) from the 2,327-member Corps of Cadets. His plea to the Corps members to help put the crazy notion into action received such a positive response that the whole student body would soon hear of it and yearn to participate.

In February 1983, *The Battalion,* Texas A&M's student paper, ran three advertisements for tryouts for the kickoff team. Sherrill and special teams coach David Beal, a former A&M quarterback, were overwhelmed by the response: At the team's first tryout, 252 Aggies (two of them women) showed up to volunteer.

Over the course of the spring and summer workouts, the team was narrowed to 17 spirited walk-ons. Sherrill's strategy—at least from a marketing standpoint—was working flawlessly. Once again, A&M made its way into *Sports Illustrated,* this time in a six-page feature in the magazine's college football preview. *New York Times* columnist George Vecsey even wrote a column about the gung ho kids in College Station.

By the time two-a-day practices had begun, skepticism was heavy among the media and even among some fans. The coaching staff, too, was beginning to worry whether Sherrill's eager gang of walk-ons could actually compete on the same field as scholarship athletes and their flashy 40-yard-dash times, even for one play. One walk-on, however, had no qualms about the group: Dennis Mudd, who drew the unenviable task of returning kickoffs in practice against the 12th Man team.

"I got tired of getting the fire knocked out of me," said Mudd, who became the kickoff team's captain in 1985. "You sensed, number one, that these guys were having a great time out there; and number two, you saw that they were great athletes. Number three is that this could happen nowhere else but at A&M."

The big day arrived on September 3, 1983. Kicker Alan Smith placed the ball for the first kickoff of the season at home (12th Man mem-bers were not allowed to play on the road because of travel squad restrictions), and the Aggie fans were, as always, on their feet. Would the California Bears—who had beaten Stanford a year earlier with "The Play," a multilateral touchdown run through the Cardinal defense and band—pull another stunt and deflate the Aggies and their newest tradition? Would the walk-ons flop, lending more ammunition to the Aggie jokesters still out there?

As Smith struck the ball off the tee, it trav-eled just six yards: Sherrill had called for an onside kick to surprise the California return team. He also didn't want to put his new highly

publicized kickoff unit under too much pressure by having to cover a long kickoff.

The Aggies recovered the kick, but California took possession because the ball hadn't gone the required 10 yards. The Bears rolled to a 17–0 lead in the game, but when the Aggies finally scored a field goal, another kickoff opportunity awaited.

The Aggies jumped all over their chance. No onside kick this time. Smith's explosive kickoff sailed two yards deep into the end zone, and Cal's Dwight Garner decided to run it out. Soon after, walk-on senior Ike Iles smacked Garner inside the 20-yard line. Kyle Field erupted.

Iles locked his hit away in his mind forever.

"I got a clean shot on him," he said. "That's something I'll be able to tell my grandchildren about."

In its first year of existence, the 12th Man Kickoff Team allowed just 13.1 yards per kickoff return, and it didn't allow a touchdown in seven home games. Sherrill's novelty had become a showcase for the spirit of Aggies everywhere, from the stands to the field.

A Fateful Touchdown by Tech

For the Aggies and their walk-on kickoff team, life was good throughout the 1980s. No opposing team had scored a touchdown on the group

The 12th Man Kickoff Team (continued)

in seven seasons. But in 1990, Texas Tech's Rodney Blackshear—who claims that on the team's flight to College Station he dreamed he broke through the 12th Man Kickoff Team for a touchdown—made his dream come true. The record was finally broken, but fortunately, his touchdown didn't cost the Aggies the game, as A&M held on to beat the Red Raiders 28–24.

But the Blackshear touchdown had major repercussions. It was an era of reduced scholarships (85 as opposed to the 95 in the 1980s) and Slocum was having difficulty fielding pol-

ished kickoff return teams for road games. These two factors led the coach to abandon the full-fledged walk-on kickoff team for a pared-down version. Since 1991, 12th Man participation has been limited to one walk-on player running down on kickoffs.

The number of 12th Man Kickoff members may have been reduced, but the enthusiasm shown by the players has been lasting. The 12th Man representative still wears the customary No. 12 jersey, he still waves his 12th man towel to the cheering maroon crowd, and he still makes some of the biggest hits of the year for the special teams.

Walk-on star Dennis Mudd summed up the spirit of the endeavor this way: "It's almost indescribable. I can't equate it to anything. To be able to get out on the field and contribute not only to the team but also to what I think of as the greatest university in the world—it was just incredible. I catch myself going back to '85 and thinking, 'Can life get this good again?' "

The 12th Man Kickoff Team *gave up just one touchdown from 1983–1990. Today, only one member of the 12th Man team runs down on kickoffs.*

Murray, Shea Walker, or Johnny Holland, and Sherrill becomes not only nostalgic but sentimental.

"There was so much potential at A&M," Sherrill says. "I looked at the school with a vision of what it was going to be like in five, ten, or twenty years. There were a lot of ingredients there to make it. A&M has no peers in loyalty, student involvement, and in giving back to the institution. Period."

From 1985 to 2001, the Aggies didn't suffer a losing season, winning 10 games or more in a season seven times. A&M owned an 11–6 edge in games with Texas over that same span.

"It was a lot of fun for me to have an opportunity to go through something like that," says Johnny Holland, an assistant coach for the Seattle Seahawks of the NFL. "I will never forget those days or that season. I'm coaching right now, and I always tell guys that no matter where you're ranked at the beginning of the season, it's all about how you finish." And it all started with a rifle-armed quarterback named Kevin Murray and a fiery coach who changed the whole mental attitude of his team and its victory-starved fans.

The Aggies finished the 1985 season like a freight train, back on track, whistle blaring.

Sherrill and then defensive coordinator R. C. Slocum hug after the big win over Auburn. It was A&M's first Cotton Bowl appearance since a 20–16 victory over Alabama in the 1968 game.

A&M won Cotton Bowl trophies in 1986 and 1988 (35–10 over Notre Dame), while losing the 1987 Classic to Ohio State 28–12.

101

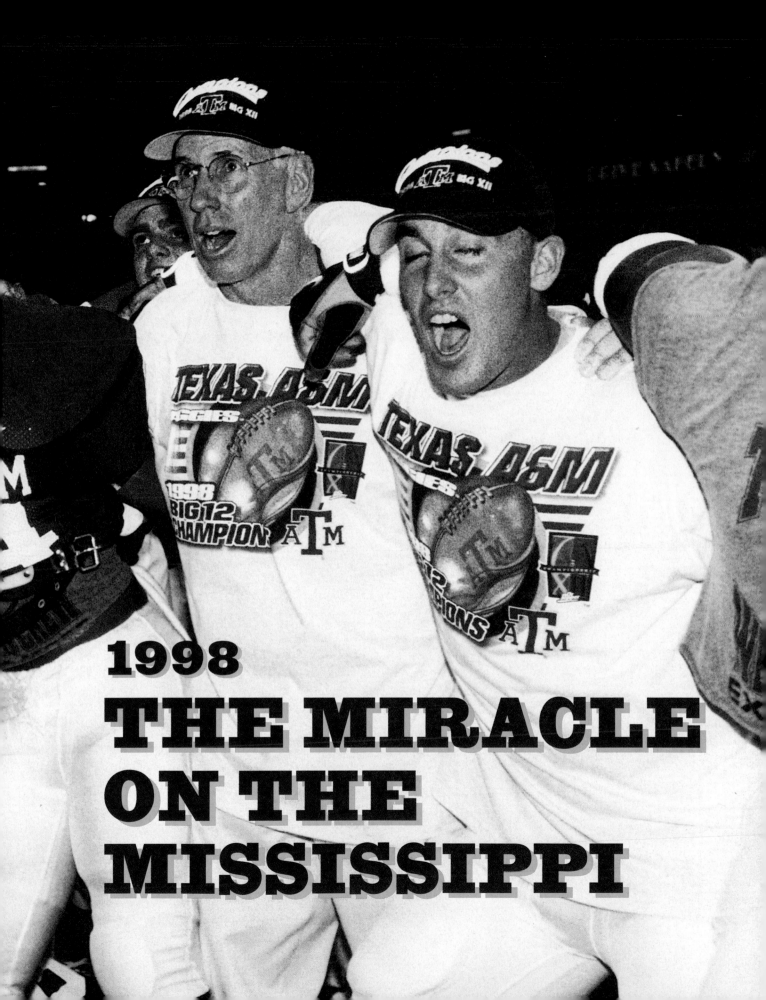

1998
THE MIRACLE
ON THE
MISSISSIPPI

Slocum's instinct about his '95 recruits proved dazzlingly correct. Parker, along with stars Dat Nguyen, Branndon Stewart, and a cast of veteran, gutsy players, would align themselves—and the planets—for one captivating season of college football.

Sirr Parker

O N THE FIRST WEDNESDAY OF FEBRUARY IN 1995—National Signing Day in college football—Texas A&M coach R. C. Slocum held a press conference to announce to the state's media the highly touted prospects he had just signed. In the middle of his address, Slocum's cell phone rang. On the other end of the line was an unfamiliar but pleasant voice that gave him even more good news: Sirr Parker, the speedy running back from Los Angeles Locke High School, volunteered that he was ready to sign his letter of intent with the Aggies. Slocum beamed with pride and excitement as his rich class of prospects hit yet another jackpot. A national championship didn't seem an impossible dream.

Three years later, Slocum's instinct about his '95 recruits proved dazzlingly correct. Parker, along with stars Dat Nguyen and Branndon Stewart, and a cast of veteran, gutsy players, would align themselves—and the planets—for one captivating season of college football. Tennessee would win the national championship, but for Texas A&M fans, 1998 was nothing but the Year of the Aggie.

Victory Dashed in a New York Minute

When Texas A&M athletic director Wally Groff and head coach R. C. Slocum accepted an invitation to play Florida State in the 1998 Kickoff Classic at Giants Stadium (across the river from Manhattan), excitement boiled over for Aggie football fans, who count the days until fall the way schoolkids yearn for the days of summer. It would be a Monday night game on national television in a stadium that featured the New York City skyline as its backdrop. What could be more perfect?

In the 1992 Cotton Bowl, 10–1 A&M and 10–2 Florida State had battled in an ugly affair. Though the Aggies dominated the game, the Seminoles pulled out a stinging 10–2 victory that had haunted A&M coaches for years; it was a loss that kept A&M from stepping onto the highest level of college football. Now, seven long years later, the Aggies had another shot at Florida State, which, along with Nebraska, had the most dominant football program of the 1990s.

Dat Nguyen

A&M was coming off a 9–4 season in 1997, having won the Big 12 Conference's South Division a year removed from a 6–6, no-bowl season of disappointment. That '96 season was the only year since 1984 that the Aggies had failed to win at least seven games. And after a 54–15 shellacking by the Nebraska Cornhuskers in the 1997 Big 12 Championship Game, the Aggies should have been wary of playing any college-football juggernaut.

But the 1998 A&M squad was blessed with experience. It not only was loaded with seasoned upperclassmen but had the fresh memory of playing against some of college football's better teams at the end of the '97 campaign—co–national champion Nebraska and red-hot UCLA. In fact, in the 1998 Cotton Bowl, the Aggies had held a 16–0 lead over the fifth-ranked Bruins—who had won nine straight games—before falling to them 29–23.

Branndon Stewart

As 59,232 fans took their seats and the Kickoff Classic began, over 500 members of the media packed the mammoth Giants Stadium press box. Most were there because the game was on a Monday night and the full regular season schedule had yet to start—but it didn't take long to get them interested.

A&M fell behind early 10–0, but the Aggies roared back with two touchdowns in the second quarter. Suddenly, when defensive back Jay Brooks scooped up a fumble by FSU quarterback Chris Weinke (who was blindsided by linebacker Christian Rodriguez) and raced to the end zone for a 21-yard touchdown return with just 29 seconds remaining before halftime, the Aggies were to be taken seriously.

By the time second-ranked Florida State and fourteenth-ranked A&M were headed to the locker room at halftime with the Aggies leading the Seminoles 14–10, a significant upset was in the works. The media buzz heightened, with writers in the press box calling editors all over the country to hold space for a possible front-page story.

The game never made it to the front page. In the third quarter, A&M's chances for the monumental victory fell to the turf after Aggie linebacker Roylin Bradley dropped a sure interception of a pass by Weinke. It was a gift-wrapped chance for Bradley, who likely would have run down an open field for a 65-yard touchdown. But after Bradley dropped the ball, Florida State kept a scoring drive alive. A&M would never recover, and FSU rallied for a 23–14 victory.

By the time second-ranked Florida State and fourteenth-ranked A&M were headed to the locker room at halftime, a significant upset was in the works. The media buzz heightened, with writers in the press box calling editors all over the country to hold space for a possible front-page story.

Still, all was not doom and gloom. Yes, the Aggies were 0–1 and had once again lost to the Seminoles. But the feeling inside both locker rooms was that A&M had a team on the verge of making some major moves on the national front.

"That's a pretty good football team we beat," Florida State coach Bobby Bowden said in the postgame press conference. "A lot of people probably expected us to blow them out, but I expect some good things from Texas A&M."

Even the cynical media were impressed by the Aggies' showing against mighty FSU, which had gained just 360 yards of total offense on 83 plays. "I think the Aggies surprised a lot of people," said television analyst Todd Blackledge.

Five weeks later, the indomitable Aggies would keep the surprises coming as the Nebraska Cornhuskers ran into the spirit of Aggieland at its most frenzied.

Clash with the Cornhuskers

After starting the 1998 season with an 0–1 record, the Aggies dispatched their next four opponents—Louisiana Tech, Southern Mississippi, North Texas, and Kansas—although none of the games were blowouts. Also, none were particularly well played because the season had seen an unusual amount of rain. The A&M offense hadn't scored more than 28 points in any of its four victories against some of the weaker teams on the schedule.

After sleepwalking through the first three quarters of the Kansas game in Lawrence, the Aggies found themselves in one of those season-making—or season-crushing—situations. Down 21–17 late in the fourth quarter, A&M went on an 11-play, 75-yard drive, capped by junior running back Dante Hall's three-yard touchdown run with 3:24 left in the game. The Aggies would pull out a 24–21 victory, but a different type of opponent awaited next week at Kyle Field. The Aggies would face second-ranked and unbeaten Nebraska, the previous season's co–national champion with Michigan.

"We can't play like we've been playing and stay on the field with Nebraska," lamented A&M coach R. C. Slocum. "The Huskers look like another verse of the same song."

Not since second-ranked Texas bowled over the Aggies 45–13 in 1983 had a team with such a lofty ranking arrived in College Station. The game had all the ingredients for a classic matchup: A&M was hell-bent on revenge after the 1997 embarrassing loss to the Cornhuskers in the Big 12 title game, and the game was at Kyle Field, where the Aggies devoured team after team in the 1990s. In fact, in that decade, A&M lost just four times at home—Texas in 1995, Colorado, Kansas State, and Texas Tech in 1996.

Kyle Field, however, would host Nebraska with only two thirds of the normal seating capacity, since construction for the stadium's massive north end zone was still underway. With a standing room–only crowd of 60,798 basking under a glorious October sun, the players took the field between the Aggie fans' sea of maroon and the Cornhuskers' bay of bright red.

The fireworks erupted early for the Aggies, with junior quarterback Randy McCown finding receiver Chris Taylor on a third-and-28 play along the Aggie sideline. Taylor took the pass that sailed over the outstretched arms of the Nebraska defender and raced 81 yards for the game's opening score. McCown would complete only two passes all day, but his only touchdown pass of the game was a welcome jolt for the 15-point underdog Aggies, now convinced that mighty Nebraska wasn't quite as dominating as it had been just 10 months before in its 13–0 season.

By the time 260-pound tailback Ja'Mar Toombs rumbled 71 yards to the Nebraska one-yard line in the second quarter, setting up the go-ahead score of 14–7 at halftime, Kyle Field was bedlam. The crowd would become even more unglued when the Aggies roared to a 28–7 lead in the third quarter.

During that stretch, the Aggie defense sacked NU quarterback Bobby Newcombe three times in three plays, and the normally explosive Husker offense had been outgained in yardage 330–117 at the end of three quarters. The proud Huskers would make a game of it in the fourth, closing the lead to 28–21. But when A&M cornerback Sedrick Curry intercepted a pass to seal the win with 51 seconds remaining, all of Aggieland rejoiced as if a huge burden was being lifted.

The Aggies had beaten No. 4 Tulane in the 1940 Sugar Bowl, No. 4 TCU in the fabled "Hurricane Game" in 1956, and No. 8 Houston in 1989. But this A&M team had scored a first by toppling No. 2 Nebraska and stopping the Huskers' 19-game overall winning streak and 40-game conference streak. Not surprisingly, the Texas A&M locker room was filled with high fives and hugs, cheers, and tears. "Tears of joy, baby," blurted senior tight end Dan Campbell, one of the Aggies' most passionate players. "There's no way you can describe this. This is why you play college football."

Nebraska defensive end Chad Kelsay had stopped Campbell on the field before the two pushed their way through the mob of players and fans and headed their separate ways. Kelsay had just a few words for Campbell and the Aggies: "Your crowd is unbelievable."

Indeed, as ABC commentator Gary Danielson said over the air-

Until he suffered *a separated shoulder in the Texas game, Randy McCown held down the quarterbacking duties in 1998.*

107

The fireworks erupted early *for the Aggies, with junior quarterback Randy McCown finding receiver Chris Taylor on a third-and-28 play along the Aggie sideline. Taylor took the pass that sailed over the outstretched arms of the Nebraska defender and raced 81 yards for the game's opening score.*

Ja'Mar Toombs (28) rumbles for a 71-yard gain to the one-yard line to break the backs of the Nebraska Cornhuskers. A&M jumped to a 28–7 lead over No. 2 Nebraska and held on for a 28–21 victory.

waves, Nebraska had just found out what Kyle Field was all about. The Cornhuskers play before some of the most knowledgeable and legendary fans in Lincoln, but even Nebraska supporters and players were in awe of the constant noise and spirit that ricochet off Kyle's towering concrete walls.

In the modern era of Aggie football, the 28–21 win over Nebraska would be considered the school's most monumental victory. Yet that notion would last for just six weeks. Red-hot Texas A&M was 5–1, with games against Texas and possibly the Big 12 title game still ahead on the schedule. The Year of the Aggie was only halfway over.

Running into Ricky

While Texas A&M had upset No. 2 Nebraska in one of the most memorable games ever played at Kyle Field, the Aggies still had to battle a pesky Texas Tech squad and push their way past a much improved Missouri team.

Against Texas Tech, the Aggies survived 17–10 when Tech's Donnie Hart hauled in a touchdown pass that would have tied the game with under a minute remaining—but Hart's feet were clearly out of bounds, nullifying the score. In another rain-soaked game at Kyle Field (four home games were played in the rain), Missouri and its talented quarterback Corby Jones were tied with the Aggies 14–14 deep into the fourth quarter. A win by A&M would give the Aggies the Big 12 South

Division title and a fitting home-field finale for seniors like inside line-backer Dat Nguyen, strong safety Rich Coady, and tight end Dan Campbell, who were playing their last game at Kyle Field.

It wasn't until a fumbled punt return by the Tigers—giving the Aggies excellent field position—that A&M had a chance to ice the victory. With 1:30 left in the game, kicker Russell Bynum booted a perfect 39-yard field goal through the rain and the uprights to notch the 17–14 victory. The Aggies had won 10 straight games and were headed to their second consecutive Big 12 title game to face top-ranked Kansas State.

But there was a hurdle along the way. As usual, all Aggie eyes turned toward the Texas game, held in Austin the day after Thanksgiving. Playing the Longhorns was always tough, made more so that year because of UT's Ricky Williams. The running back was en route to an NCAA record of 6,279 career rushing yards and the 1998 Heisman Trophy. His performance against the Aggies would go down as one of the most dazzling individual performances in the history of the Aggie-Longhorn series.

When the Aggies took the field in Austin, high drama was once again the order of the day. Former Heisman Trophy winners like Pittsburgh's Tony Dorsett, Texas's Earl Campbell, and A&M's John David Crow walked the side-lines in anticipation of Williams breaking Dorsett's all-time rushing mark, and a national television audience was tuning in.

When Williams broke through the Aggie line of scrim-mage in the second quarter and dashed into history with a 60-yard touchdown run that set the new NCAA yardage mark, most of the 83,687 fans inside Darrell K. Royal Memorial Stadium could hardly contain themselves. Play was halted as Williams received congratulations from Dorsett and even John David Crow.

By game's end, Williams had run over and around the Aggies for 259 rushing yards on 44 attempts. Yet against all odds, with the 7–3 Longhorns leading 23–7 with 9:46 left in the game, the Aggies showed the heart and grit that had characterized this team all season long. Remembering the close games and rallies to beat Kansas, Texas Tech, and Missouri, A&M reeled off a shocking 17 straight points after being out of the game for three quarters. When quarterback Randy McCown busted through the Texas defense on an option keeper for a one-yard touchdown on fourth down, A&M had an inconceivable 24–23 lead with 2:20 left in the game.

But victory would not be theirs. Texas and quarterback Major Applewhite would take advantage of a soft A&M prevent defense and drive the length of the field to set up a game-winning 24-yard field goal

In the modern era of Aggie football, the 28–21 win over Nebraska would be considered the school's most monumental victory . . . at least for six weeks.

On Aggie shoulders, *R. C. Slocum is carried across Kyle Field after the emotional win over Nebraska.*

with five seconds left in the contest. Texas won the heart-pounding game 26–24 as its superstar tailback took over the top spot in the NCAA history books and solidified his place atop the race for the Heisman Trophy. (Williams's record would last just one season, however. Wisconsin's Ron Dayne would top the charts the following fall with 6,397 career rushing yards.)

For Texas A&M, it was another painful loss to the Longhorns. "We had to fight back so hard to get back to the top of the mountain," a teary-eyed McCown said after the game. "To get all the way back, take the lead and then lose . . . it's just a real hard pill to swallow." But the hurt would linger for just a day or two. The Aggies had more work to do, facing an 11–0 Kansas State team for the Big 12 championship on December 5, 1998. Most of the nation yawned at the idea of 10–2 A&M, a 15-point underdog, taking on the unbeaten and seemingly unbeatable Wildcats. The Aggies, however, were soon to issue a wake-up call that would shake up college football.

Randy McCown and the Aggies nearly stunned Texas in the regular season finale, roaring back from a 23–7 deficit in the fourth quarter to take a 24–23 lead. But they were unable to stop the Longhorns' downfield march to the heartbreaking, game-winning field goal.

Bad News from the Beginning

Not only had Texas A&M fallen short against Texas, stopping a 10-game winning streak, but starting quarterback Randy McCown had suffered a separated shoulder on the touchdown run that gave A&M their brief lead. Making things even more difficult was the fact that the Big 12 Championship Game was to be played in St. Louis, where a mass of purple-clad KSU fans had traveled east in hopes of experiencing one more coronation for their Wildcats. The fans were all the more revved up because KSU was once considered to have the worst program in Division I football.

Ranked No. 1 in the *USA Today* coaches poll but third in the Bowl Championship Series (BCS) standings, the Wildcats needed a UCLA loss to Miami that day, coupled with a win in the Big 12 title game, to get to the Fiesta Bowl for a crack at the national championship. Only the banged-up Aggies—who had been battered by the Wildcats 36–17 the year before in Manhattan, Kansas—stood in the way.

The A&M defense was a solid one, led by Dat Nguyen. Along with linebackers Warrick Holdman and Roylin Bradley, the Aggies were a tough group to break down. The Aggie offense, however, was hardly dynamic, topping the 30-point scoring mark (a 35–14 win over lowly Baylor) just once all season long. With Randy McCown's shoulder now in a sling and Branndon Stewart handling the quarterback duties, there were more unanswered questions entering this game than at any other time since the season had started.

Stewart had shown flashes of living up to his early newspaper clippings. He had rallied the troops to nearly beat Brigham Young University in his first game as an Aggie in 1996, and his fourth-quarter passing exhibition that brought A&M from behind to beat Oklahoma State in 1997 was a classic performance. When McCown was injured in the 1998 Oklahoma State game, Stewart fired a touchdown pass on his first play from scrimmage to spark the Aggies to a 17–6 win. Still, Stewart had lost his starting job in 1998. Could he handle the pressure of the spotlight, especially against this kind of opponent?

Once the game against Kansas State got under way, it looked as though Stewart wouldn't last for even a quarter. The Aggie quarterback suffered a hyperextended knee and writhed in pain on the floor of the TWA Dome. Not only were the Aggies heavy underdogs to a talented KSU team led by all-world quarterback Michael Bishop but now A&M appeared to be saddled with not one, but two injured quarterbacks. The rout, it appeared, had begun.

The situation was so dire that punter Shane Lechler was told by the A&M coaches to get ready to quarterback. Lechler had been a high school quarterback at East Bernard (Texas) High School before he became an All-America punter at Texas A&M— but even so, his abilities were limited. He knew just six pass plays and was actually about to

"We had to fight back so hard to get back to the top of the mountain," a teary-eyed McCown said after the game. "To get all the way back, take the lead and then lose . . . it's just a real hard pill to swallow."

Texas A&M had faced a 15-point deficit before, rallying to beat Oklahoma State in overtime in 1997. The Aggies would remember that hard-fought game as they struggled to overtake Kansas State in the Big 12 title game.

take the field with his punting shoe still on. With a patchwork offensive line also bitten by injuries (starting right tackle Andy Vincent had gone down with a knee injury), this was code blue for the maroon and white.

Amazingly, Stewart's knee felt better as he loosened it up along the sideline. Fortunately for the Aggies, Lechler remained strictly on punting duties and Stewart returned to the game, adrenaline taking over as his best medicine.

The Tide Begins to Turn

With the Aggies trailing 17–6 at halftime—and the 60,798 fans fully aware that UCLA had lost to Miami earlier in the day, thus clearing the way to the national title game for KSU—the Wildcats and their supporters began looking ahead, too far ahead, in fact. Some Wildcat fans were already on cell phones booking plane reservations for Tempe, Arizona, site of the Tostitos Fiesta Bowl.

The Wildcat players did indeed look confident in the third quarter, extending their lead to 27–12 with 15 minutes left on the clock. But those 15 minutes would become a lifetime for KSU.

Kansas State had won just once from 1987 to 1989, racking up 31 losses in the process. But once coach Bill Snyder was able to import more junior college transfers and land players such as Michael Bishop, the Wildcats soared to the top of college football. In fact, no other program had risen so far so dramatically as KSU. And now the Wildcats just needed to keep Texas A&M at bay for 15 measly minutes.

But the Aggies would not go away—and would not quit. Instead, they turned up the heat in the fourth quarter. And Branndon Stewart had found his rhythm.

It had taken three quarters to fully utilize the strategy, but A&M coaches, opposing coaches, and even ABC commentator Dan Fouts all agreed that the best way to beat KSU was to throw the ball into the teeth of a suspect KSU secondary. Stewart obliged, finding tight end Derrick Spiller across the middle on several big plays. After Stewart hit receiver Leroy Hodge in the end zone for a 13-yard touchdown pass, A&M cut into the Wildcats' lead 27–19. Still, there were more big plays needed—and quickly. The time for a historic comeback was waning.

With just under three minutes remaining in the game, the Aggies caught their first big break. On third-and-4, linebacker Warrick Holdman blindsided Michael Bishop on a quarterback keeper, forcing a fumble after Bishop had secured a game-sealing first down. It was A&M linebacker Cornelius Anthony who outfought Bishop for the ball at the KSU 35-yard line. "That was the story of our season," safety Rich Coady said. "Different people always stepped up when we needed the big play."

It was time for Stewart to work some more magic. And he did. His nine-yard touchdown pass to Sirr Parker cut the lead to 29–27 with 1:05

The Wildcats just needed to keep Texas A&M at bay for 15 measly minutes. But the Aggies would not go away—and would not quit. Instead, they turned up the heat in the fourth quarter.

Branndon Stewart: The Comeback Kid

In the early 1990s, Branndon Stewart was a football phenomenon in the so-called Dairy Capital of Texas—the sleepy little town of Stephenville.

At the University of Tennessee, he became the heir apparent to the starting quarterback job, only to see that dream dissipate into backup duty behind superstar quarterback Peyton Manning. Longing for playing time and life in his home state, Stewart transferred to Texas A&M in the spring of 1995. There were equal parts hype and hope for Stewart, whom the Aggies proclaimed the next quarterback savior in maroon and white.

But A&M would have to wait for its miracle. In his first two games as a starter to open the 1996 season, A&M lost to both Brigham Young and Southwestern Louisiana. The BYU game ended on a Stewart fumble. The Southwestern Louisiana game deteriorated into an embarrassing loss, as Stewart threw four interceptions (two for touch-

downs) in a 29–22 debacle. It wasn't until the 1998 defeat of Kansas State that Stewart would find his ultimate redemption.

Despite the rough start to his Aggie career and being benched for his senior year, Stewart finished his college career in style. He now lives in Austin working as a systems engineer for a high-technology company, but he returns to A&M often as one of its most successful student-athlete graduates. And anyone who sees him usually brings up the 1998 thriller against Kansas State.

"I would say probably ninety percent of the Aggies I meet—they try to keep it from being the first thing out of their mouth, but it's the second thing—say that was the best game they've ever seen," Stewart says. "I guess when I'm seventy-five, I'll be talking to people who will say, 'Hey, great to meet you. A&M is a great school, and that was the greatest game I've ever seen.'"

Suddenly, amazingly, Texas A&M and Kansas State were tied. Stadium workers who had lugged huge boxes of T-shirts commemorating KSU's surefire victory were all of a sudden running for those marked TEXAS A&M.

remaining, and Parker would haul in the game-tying two-point conversion just seconds later.

Suddenly, amazingly, Texas A&M and Kansas State were tied. Stadium workers who had lugged huge boxes of T-shirts commemorating KSU's surefire victory were all of a sudden running for those marked TEXAS A&M.

Along the sidelines, K-State players fidgeted nervously. A&M players, meanwhile, were hamming it up with coach R. C. Slocum as if this were a game of two-hand touch against some kids at the corner park. "Once we got it tied," Dan Campbell remembers, "there was no way we were going to let it slip away."

But it almost did. Bishop's Hail Mary pass toward the end zone with no time left was caught at the one-yard line by Everett Burnett. A&M safety Toya Jones made a game-saving tackle, sending the game into overtime.

Sirr Parker on the Slant

For the game, Dat Nguyen had posted 17 tackles against Kansas State and recorded an interception, while Stewart had torched the KSU defense for 235 passing yards in the fourth quarter alone. But Sirr Parker, the sometimes disconsolate, sometimes dazzling tailback from the West Coast, was about to etch his name into A&M history books with one miraculous catch-and-run to the corner of the end zone.

Parker had chosen Texas A&M in part because he wanted to play as far away from the gang-infested district of South Central Los Angeles as he possibly could. For three seasons, he had been solid

Sirr Parker: Up from the Streets

The life of Sirr Parker is the stuff movies are made of—in his case, literally. In 2000, Showtime produced *They Call Him Sirr*, the story of California-born Parker's rise from the mean streets of South Central Los Angeles to football glory.

The child of alcoholics, Parker was raised by his grandmother. His mother returned years later with another son, then promptly left again.

A child himself, Parker divided his time between the football field and taking care of his little brother, Donyea. While drug dealers and gangbangers were ruling the streets, Sirr was making his mark on the field: In his senior year of high school, he rushed 1,129 yards and scored 19 touchdowns, even though his team went 0–9.

Parker was recruited by Notre Dame, UCLA, Washington, and Arizona, but chose Texas A&M because it was closer to Houston, where Donyea had recently moved in with an aunt.

"Kids are innocent, and don't ask to be here," Parker told a *Cincinnati Enquirer* reporter in August 2000. "I have to do what I can to take care of him. Those were the type of morals I was raised with by my grandmother."

After his stint in the NFL, Parker bounced around the Canadian Football League and played for the Cincinnati Bengals. But his legend in football points directly back to that Big 12 championship night in St. Louis, when he outran the Kansas State Wildcats to the corner of the end zone.

Dat Nguyen: Defying the Stereotype

During his career at A&M, Dat Nguyen racked up 517 tackles—a school record. The former Rockport-Fulton product became an Aggie legend from 1994–98, winning the 1998 Lombardi Award as the nation's top lineman on either side of the ball and becoming the Big 12 Conference's Defensive Player of the Year. He also won the Chuck Bednarik Award as the country's premier defensive player. As a fantastic football player and an even more likable person, he became a local folk hero for A&M fans and a role model for other Asian Americans. But the road to glory wasn't easy.

Nguyen was born in an Arkansas refugee camp in 1975, after his Vietnamese family had escaped a war-torn homeland in a boat as bombs fell over their country. He admits to being a troublemaker as a child, but credits football for turning him around.

"Football was my salvation," said Nguyen in 1998. "I was always getting in trouble. But football helped me mature. I'm lucky I started playing when I did."

Still, he arrived in Aggieland in 1994 as an unhappy, pudgy, and homesick kid. Redshirted for the 1994 season, he even thought about leaving school and going home.

In the spring of 1995, Nguyen began to lose weight and gain confidence as a player. Not only did his career take off, but his stature in the community blossomed as well. As a fantastic football player and an exceptionally likable person, Nguyen became a folk hero for A&M fans and a role model for other Asian Americans who could follow this rare athlete's exploits on and off the field.

In College Station, Nguyen spoke often at elementary schools. At one, he befriended a young Vietnamese student, Quang Pham, who was adjusting slowly to American life. Speaking almost no English and reading at a kindergarten level, the fifth-grader was hesitant to participate in class discussions. But Nguyen visited Pham once a week throughout the semester, helping the young, shy student increase his reading level—and class involvement—threefold.

On the field as a professional player, Nguyen became the first player of Asian descent to make an NFL roster. He joined the Dallas Cowboys, and in 2002 signed a six-year, $13.5 million extension with the team. But for all of his football talents, Nguyen's impact at Texas A&M goes beyond the realm of football.

Says A&M coach R. C. Slocum, "Look at the way Dat's handled his success and what he's done off the field to try to make his community and his world a better place. He's just an exceptional young man, and Texas A&M was fortunate to have him."

Dat Nguyen and Randy McCown
celebrate a big play in the '98 season.

117

Tailback Sirr Parker *takes a quick slant pass from Branndon Stewart and starts his sprint to the corner of the end zone.*

Parker keeps *the Kansas State defender at bay long enough to stretch over the goal line for the game-winning touchdown in double overtime. The Aggies had rallied from 15 points down to shock not only No. 1 KSU but the world of college football.*

but hardly spectacular. On this day, his play so far had been the highlight of an injury-filled senior year. But fate and a quick slant pass would change Parker's legacy forever.

In the first two overtime possessions, A&M swapped field goals with Kansas State. After the A&M defense rose up and forced another K-State field goal to push the score to 33–30 in favor of the Wildcats, the Aggies took over with hopes of sending the game into a third overtime.

But after a penalty pushed A&M kicker Russell Bynum out of his comfort zone at the 32-yard line, and facing a third-and-17, the play came in from the Aggie sideline. It would be similar to the slant pass to Parker that had pulled the Aggies to within 27–25 earlier in the game. Offensive coordinator Steve Kragthorpe called the play in hopes of just picking up eight or nine yards to move Bynum closer in for a field goal try.

Just before the snap of the ball, Kansas State adjusted their defense—in A&M's favor—by moving a cornerback out on Parker; a safety had been used earlier. But when Stewart hit Parker between a frozen linebacker and the overplaying cornerback, Parker split the seam and raced toward the corner of the end zone. A&M had recruited Parker for his 4.3 speed in the 40-yard dash—and he needed every last bit to jet to the pylon.

Parker was tackled right at the pylon, but the official—who was in a good position to make the call—ruled that the ball had crossed the plane of the goal line before Parker's knee hit the ground. The game was over.

Sirr Parker and the Aggies had just shocked KSU 36–33 in two overtimes, turning the world of college football on its head in one quick slant pass down the gut of the Wildcat defense. Parker was mobbed on the field by teammates, Yell Leaders, and A&M officials. R. C. Slocum danced with his players at midfield, and fans of both schools cried in the stands.

Still in the press box atop the stadium, offensive coordinator Steve Kragthorpe dropped to the ground in exhaustion and jubilation. "I fell to my knees and said, 'Thank you, Jesus,' " Kragthorpe recalled. "It was a miracle—a miracle finish."

> ### Did You Know?
> Texas A&M had never beaten a team ranked first or second in any major poll in the history of the football program. In 1998, the Aggies pulled the trick twice, beating second-ranked Nebraska and top-ranked Kansas State.
>
> Since that devastating upset for Kansas State, the Wildcats lost subsequent games to A&M in 2000 (26–10) and 2001 (31–24).

Leroy Hodge (88) and teammates celebrate the touchdown that began A&M's improbable comeback in the fourth quarter.

Celebration in College Station

Texas A&M had beaten No. 2 Nebraska earlier in the season, and now the 11–2 Aggies had taken down the top-ranked Wildcats for the Big 12 title. They had also gained a berth in the Nokia Sugar Bowl opposite

Hordes of A&M fans gathered at College Station's Easterwood Airport at midnight to welcome home coach R. C. Slocum and his Big 12 champions.

Every Aggie football fan had a story of where he or she watched the incredible events of December 5, 1998, unfold.

Ohio State, which had spent 10 weeks atop the college polls before a November loss to Michigan State. The shocking events of the Aggie-Wildcat game echoed throughout the country on that December day in St. Louis, as college football's bowl scenario was rocked on its heels. With Tennessee winning the Southeastern Conference title later that night, the Volunteers would now play—and later beat—Florida State for the national title in the Fiesta Bowl.

Kansas State University, meanwhile, stumbled all the way down to the Alamo Bowl, a small consolation prize for a team so close to playing for it all.

The Wildcats had come so far, from the depths of college football to a few inches from the mountaintop.

The 1998 Big 12 title was the Aggies' first conference crown since they topped the SWC in 1993.

But they had played close to the vest in the second half against the Aggies and, undoubtedly, played not to lose in the overtime periods. A&M, on the other hand, had played to win, perhaps taking a lesson from their soft defensive strategies in the 26–24 loss to Texas a week earlier.

While the hamlet of Manhattan, Kansas, was slipping into a funk, the celebrations in the state of Texas were just beginning. Car horns and hullabaloo blared through the streets of College Station. Every Aggie football fan had a story of where he or she watched the incredible events of December 5, 1998, unfold. And everyone remembered how A&M radio announcer Dave South had screamed, "He got a touchdown! He got a touchdown!" over the radio airwaves.

At College Station's Easterwood Airport, fans began gathering to greet the team two hours before the Aggie charter landed at midnight. It was a maroon mob scene reminiscent of the Northgate parties that broke out in 1984 and 1985 after the big wins over Texas. But there was a feeling that this victory was indeed bigger than any that had gone before.

The Aggies would end the 1998 season ranked eleventh after a 24–14 loss to Ohio State in the Sugar Bowl. But that disappointment hardly took the wind out of their sails. After all, A&M had beaten No. 1 Kansas State in such dramatic fashion that many considered it the game of the year in college football.

The curtain really closed on the unforgettable 1998 season before the Sugar Bowl. The season had opened with the near-win with Florida State and progressed to the picture-perfect day against Nebraska at Kyle Field. Later, the Aggies costarred in the Ricky Williams show in Austin. In the end, it was left to tail-back Sirr Parker to take the curtain call in St. Louis, with a touchdown for the ages.

Dat Nguyen capped an amazing career at A&M by winning the Lombardi and Chuck Bednarik awards as the nation's top defensive player.

LOMBARDI AWARD

DAT NGUYEN

Sounding Off

"I'm just happy for everyone involved with Texas A&M University. This is the kind of win that transcends football. It speaks highly of the whole university and the character and values of this university: To be able to come back, stick to our guns, and make the plays down the stretch."

—*A&M offensive coordinator Steve Kragthorpe (1997–2000)*

AGGIE BONFIRE
THE SPIRIT BURNS ON

Since 1909, Aggies had gathered around some form of fir—originally nothing more than a burning trash heap—to bond, to reminisce, and to show en masse that their school and their spirit had no rival.

TO ANYONE PASSING THROUGH COLLEGE STATION on a late November afternoon, the sight was comfortingly familiar: There, strikingly visible over the distant oak trees lining the campus, was the autumn landmark, towering against the sky.

Two colors clashed at the top of the six-tiered stack of logs that made up the landmark: the colors of a burnt-orange outhouse—representing a fraternity house at the University of Texas—and a bright green Austin City Limits sign. This was Aggie Bonfire, a mighty and unmistakable beacon to Texas A&M fans arriving for the annual football game with the Longhorns.

Since 1909, Aggies had gathered around some form of fire—originally nothing more than a burning trash heap—to bond, to reminisce, and to show en masse that their school and their spirit had no rival.

For lovers of the maroon and white, this annual pilgrimage to Aggieland wasn't about seeing logs burn. The saying goes that Bonfire symbolized the undying Aggie spirit and the "burning desire to beat the hell outta TU." (Aggies like to think "the" university in Texas resides in College Station, and "Texas" University is that school over in Austin.)

But Bonfire was more than just a big pep rally, or in Aggie nomenclature, yell practice. It had come to represent the special feeling Aggies have for working together, building friendships, and going the extra mile—or, if need be, a hundred—to be true to their school.

The Aggies built Bonfire every year for 53 years straight, until 1963. That November, President John F. Kennedy was assassinated, and A&M students decided to dismantle Bonfire in an act of mourning and respect for their slain president.

From 1964 to 1998, Bonfire sparked again, bigger and brighter than ever. In 1969, the tallest bonfire ever built anywhere (so says the Guinness Book of Records) shot 109 feet into the sky. And through the decades of the '80s and '90s, the wedding cake–shaped stack of 6,000 logs continued as a one-of-a-kind leadership forum, a student-run rite of passage that could have taken shape only on this spirited campus.

Then, at 2:42 in the morning on November 18, 1999, Aggie Bonfire collapsed, killing 12 students and injuring 27. It was the darkest moment in Texas A&M history.

With grief in their hearts, Aggies reached out for one another. In the end, the Aggie spirit manifested itself like never before and helped heal a school struggling to understand why this spirited tradition—idolized by so many innocent students—could result in such tragedy.

From Trash Pile to Towering Stack

In its early years, Aggie Bonfire was nothing more than a garbage fire, as students gathered up any combustible items of trash they could find for their on-campus campfires. Before important football games and other big sporting events, the Corps of Cadets would ignite these rudimentary bonfires to incite more of the trademark Aggie spirit that reverberated through the campus. Anything was fair game: In 1912, for instance, Cadets "acquired" lumber being used for the construction of Milner and Legett Halls for their crude bonfires.

A few days of work resulted in a mound of refuse to rally around. But Aggies became increasingly innovative in their quest for camaraderie—and after complaints from area farmers about wood and other materials disappearing from their properties, the university stepped in and allowed only fresh-cut logs to be used. By 1943, a stack of wood 25 feet high burned into the night before the annual football bloodletting with the University of Texas.

The 1945 Bonfire was the first to use logs in a tepee shape. The earliest Bonfires were merely heaps of trash and wood.

125

Senior Red Pots lead Elephant Walk—the last parade around campus for the senior class.

The Bonfires of the 1950s, '60s and '70s were tepee-style stacks of wood, and Yell Leaders were the main organizers of the ever growing event. By 1954, Bonfire stood 73 feet high, and in 1969 Aggie Bonfire had ballooned into a 109-foot colossus of logs from trees that had been cleared from area landholdings.

Concerned with the world-record height of the '69 flames, fire marshals and A&M officials appeased neighboring homeowners in 1970 and protected the school's physical plant by limiting the height of Bonfire to 55 feet and its width to 45 feet. The circumference of the stack could total 195 feet.

By the early 1980s, the height and breadth of Bonfire would take on new and dynamic dimensions. The tepee style was replaced by the familiar wedding cake look—six stacks of wood, shrinking in size as they went up, topped off by the orange outhouse. A center pole (the first was erected in 1946) made of two telephone poles spliced together anchored the towering structure.

A Bonfire hierarchy of organizers had grown out of this burgeoning subculture of student worker bees (construction responsibilities had been taken over from the Yell Leaders in the late 1960s). The protective helmets the students wore while working on the stack designated their rung on the leadership ladder. Junior and senior "Red Pots" were the highest-ranking students—the decisionmakers and fund-raisers; most of the equipment was donated, but Red Pots still had to raise $50,000 annually to help cover costs. "Brown Pots" handled equipment safety and site logistics, while "Yellow Pots" coordinated all the workers from the dorms. Female "Pink Pots" organized any women (first allowed on the cut site in 1979) who were ready to lend a helping hand to the project.

But with this extensive student network—and the students' desire to build Bonfire bigger and badder in each successive year—the university's announcement of regulations for the height and width of the stack fell on deaf ears. In fact, it was common knowledge that the Bonfire stack had soared far higher than 55 feet over the last 15 to 20 years.

While expertise and safety precautions were passed down annually from each group of Red Pots to the next in line and A&M engineers offered con-

Did You Know?

Students from arch rival University of Texas attempted to prematurely light Bonfire on several occasions. In 1933 and 1948, firebombs were even dropped from a plane; in 1956, small explosives were planted in the stack. None of the attempts were successful.

The 1969 stack shot 109 feet into the sky to set a world record for the height of a bonfire.

struction tips, there was never a defining blueprint of engineering instruction developed for Aggie Bonfire.

Ultimately, a combination of spotty university supervision, design flaws, poor site location, and bad luck melded into one. The result was a doomed—and deadly—1999 Bonfire.

The Camaraderie of "Cut"

To understand an Aggie's fervor for Bonfire takes more than just witnessing the lighting of the big fire the night before the Texas game (or two nights before whenever the game is in Austin). Bonfire's grip on the 5,000 students who labored on it each fall was a result of the 125,000 man-hours spent working together on the massive project. It was about coming together when students on so many other campuses seemed to go their separate ways.

Beginning the first weekend of October and continuing through mid-November, A&M students sacrificed their weekends for the gathering of wood. As early as five in the morning, students would awaken to the Bonfire organizers pounding ax handles on doors, steel light standards, or any other noise-producing object in the vicinity.

Did You Know?

Texas A&M students gathered wood for Bonfire by helping clear private land-holdings, but Aggies also gave back. Every year, thousands of students from 50 different organizations replanted the cut site with 10,000 seedlings.

Members of the Corps of Cadets haul logs out of the woods to the truck-loading site. The white tape around their legs identifies first-timers to the cut site.

Exhausted workers take a break after cutting down trees with axes. A&M students would sacrifice their weekends to work at the cut site for two months before Bonfire burned.

To work on the stack, students had to hang in swings as they wired logs together. A crane donated by a generous Aggie helped carry logs to the higher levels of Aggie Bonfire.

While parties at other schools were just winding down, wake-up calls and doughnut runs at Texas A&M were just beginning. Students piled into pickup trucks, heading off to land tracts in the thick central Texas woods. Aggie Band music blared from cassette decks during the 30-minute drive, and the message rang clear with each pulsating song: This was crazy, totally foreign, and Aggieland at its finest.

Students from each dorm and Corps of Cadets outfit walked into the forest to join what was called cut. They carried canteens of water and axes (chain saws were used only for clearing and trimming trees), and city slickers and Paul Bunyan wannabes joined forces to cut down the hardwood oak trees that surround the College Station landscape. Trees fell at a steady pace, and it was grinding, backbreaking work. The ax swinging continued into the late afternoon. Then, as students carried trees out to the perimeter of the site to be loaded onto trucks for the drive back to A&M, there was an incredible sense of pride and accomplishment. Bonfire would burn two months later, but the journey—not the destination—would create the most lasting memories.

Back on the campus stack site—first Simpson Drill Field until 1955, then Duncan Field until 1992, and finally the roomier polo fields on the opposite side of campus—logs were unloaded and stacked in piles as prepping grounds for the actual building of the bonfire.

Once the center pole was hauled in on October 30, work would continue on the stack for a month. Using donated cranes, tractors, and pulley systems to lift logs, students would hang in wooden "swings" on

the stack to guide the logs into place. The trimmed trees were then fastened to one another with baling wire.

"Push" would mark the final countdown, with students working in six-hour shifts 24 hours a day for 10 days straight. At "dark-thirty" in Aggie Bonfire time (usually around 8 p.m.) on the night before a Texas game in College Station, 50,000 to 70,000 onlookers—including pods of Longhorn fans—would gather around the stack, which was doused with 700 gallons of diesel fuel for lighting.

As the Aggie Band paraded around Bonfire, the Yell Leaders and Red Pots followed with the torches that would be launched onto the six stacks of wood. The fire that erupted seemed to light up all of Brazos County. Aggies held their customary yell practice and the Head Yell Leader then read aloud the traditional poem, "The Last Corps Trip."

In the years before the tragedy, close to 50,000 people would encircle Aggie Bonfire, which was lit by torches carried by the Yell Leaders and Red Pots. The legend goes that if a burning Bonfire stood past midnight, the Aggies would be victorious over the Longhorns the following day.

Goose bumps formed—as they always did at Bonfire—under every Aggie jacket out there.

"A Horrible, Horrible Accident"

The early morning hours of November 18, 1999 were buzzing with activity. It was Push week, with Aggie Bonfire set to be lit on November 25. Fifty or more students straddled their swings on the stack, climbed up and down the logs, and barked commands to fellow workers in Aggie lingo.

Men, women, seniors, freshmen, even former students—the entire Aggie community was represented on the stack that night. Then, at just past 2:30 in the morning, the 40-foot stack began to shift and sink.

Bonfire had fallen before, in 1994, when incessant rains pounded College Station for a week. The drainage grounds of the polo fields had become waterlogged, and a shifting stack slowly leaned over and eventually toppled to the ground. But that year, no one had been on stack at the time. Hindsight says the accident should have been a wake-up call for A&M—but instead, a mass of diligent Aggie students took the stack apart and rebuilt it in a week. It was considered one of the high points of recent Bonfires in terms of work ethic and construction.

> ### Did You Know?
> Texas A&M football players decided as a group to skip football practice the day of the tragedy. Coach R. C. Slocum concurred, and the team went to the site to offer whatever help they could. Players were soon covered in sawdust and dirt as they carried off many of the larger logs surrounding the stack so that rescue workers could better maneuver in the area.
>
> "Sometimes you lose the whole perspective of what Texas A&M is all about," said All-America punter Shane Lechler. "When this tragedy happened and we were able to go out there and help with the clearing of logs at the site, it brought this team back into the perspective that this is the most special school in the country."

The Bonfire stack collapsed at 2:42 a.m., as students were working the early morning shift during Push week. Some students were trapped for hours in the heap of thousands of logs, and 12 would not survive.

But this time, the collapse was different. The stack was crawling with students, and there was no time to escape.

Suddenly, the grinding and splintering of wood pierced the perimeter. Bonfire was coming down, spiraling to the ground in a catastrophic fall. Some students rode the logs down to the ground like surfers skimming a big swell. Others fell hard to the ground, snapping their limbs on contact.

The majority of the students made it through the harrowing seconds alive. But 12 Aggies did not. Some, like Tim Kerlee, were trapped in a pile of logs weighing tons. Pinned but still alert, Kerlee directed rescue workers to other injured students before succumbing to the crushing injuries himself. (Kerlee would make it out of the stack alive, but after battling severe internal injuries for 48 hours, he became the twelfth Aggie to die from the collapse.) Kerlee, just 17 years old, had been living out his dream of being an Aggie freshman in the Corps for just three months.

With Bonfire crumpled into a massive heap, word began to spread among the Aggie community and the nation at large. A tragedy of huge proportions had stunned the Texas A&M campus.

"It was a horrible, horrible accident," said Carl Baggett, the head Red Pot back in 1996

and student-body president in 1997. "I was just in shock. I couldn't believe that those great students out there having fun and volunteering for A&M had lost their lives."

As hordes of rescue teams swarmed over the stack, students sat grimly on the outskirts, crying, hugging, and praying. Parents and friends of the university flooded phone lines trying to reach their loved ones. Satellite television trucks from all over the state filled the parking lots next to the site, and national network anchors led their broadcasts with the sad news.

By the afternoon of November 18, exhausted rescue workers had removed all of the bodies from the stack, and the reports were grave. Eleven Aggies had perished in the collapse: Miranda Adams, Christopher Breen, Michael Ebanks, Jeremy Frampton, Jamie Hand, Christopher Heard, Lucas Kimmel, Bryan McClain, Chad Powell, Jerry Self, and Nathan West. Freshman Tim Kerlee succumbed to internal injuries two days later. A thirteenth victim, John Comstock, would remain in critical condition for weeks before ultimately surviving the ordeal.

News crews from all over the state of Texas swarmed over the Bonfire site, which was quickly becoming a makeshift memorial for the Aggies who were victims of the disastrous collapse.

Coming Together in Mourning

An absolutely stunned and disconsolate Texas A&M campus, which had fostered so many fine traditions over the years, was now having to deal with pure tragedy. The Aggies had been strong

Grieving Aggies *left many mementos around the Bonfire perimeter. Some mourners even placed their cherished Aggie Rings at the base of the main flagpole near the Bonfire site.*

before, especially in wartime, when many Cadets had given their lives for their country.

But this seemed so inexplicable, so unthinkable.

"This has been a day of unspeakable grief and sorrow," said A&M president Dr. Ray Bowen. "Our sorrow is great. Our pain is deep. Our suffering is immense. We must continue to support one another during these difficult times."

Indeed, the support would be overwhelming. At a memorial service the night of November 18, over 12,000 Aggies and even some Longhorns gathered at A&M's special events center, Reed Arena, to pray together and pay tribute to the fallen students.

Former President George Bush, whose presidential library sits just to the west of the arena, was in attendance, as was then Lieutenant Governor Rick Perry, a 1972 graduate and former Yell Leader (Perry became governor of Texas when George W. Bush moved into the White House in 2001). Perry's words of remembrance would reverberate among the grief-stricken crowd.

University of Texas student-body president Eric Opiela was part of a Longhorn contingent who made the 100-mile trek to College Station to offer condolences at the memorial service. He was overtaken by the Aggie spirit that night, prompting him to write a poignant letter to the A&M student newspaper, *The Battalion:*

"The A&M student body is truly one of the great treasures of our state. As part of the UT delegation, we sat on the floor of Reed Arena and immediately following the end of the service I heard this rustling sound behind me. I looked over my shoulder and saw the sight of close to 20,000 students spontaneously putting their arms on their neighbor's shoulders, forming a great circle around the arena.

"The mass stood there in pin-drop silence for close to five minutes; then, from somewhere, someone began to hum quietly the hymn 'Amazing Grace.' Within seconds, the whole arena was singing. I tried, too—I choked, I cried. This event brought me to tears. It was one of—if not the—defining moment of my college career. I learned something tonight: For all us Longhorns to discount A&M in our never-ending rivalry, we need to realize one thing—Aggieland is a special place, with special people.

"It is infinitely better equipped than we are at dealing with tragedy such as this for one simple reason. It is a family. It is a family that cares for its own, a family that reaches out, a family that is unified in the face of adversity, a family that moved this Longhorn to tears.

"My heart, my prayers, and the heart of the UT student body go out tonight to Aggies and their families and friends as they recover from this great loss. Texas A&M, The Eyes of Texas are Upon You—and they look with sincere sympathy upon a family that has been through so much tragedy this semester."

"We will remember them," Perry said of the Bonfire victims, "as long as there is a Texas A&M and the Aggie spirit lives. And that, my friends, is forever."

In the days following the accident, while funerals for the fallen Aggie 12 were being held, Texas A&M and Aggie Bonfire became the leading topic of conversation in College Station, in Texas, and perhaps the country. And people around the world tuned in to CNN to follow the terrible story.

President Bill Clinton sent his condolences, and then Governor George W. Bush, in the midst of his presidential campaign, offered his support in a heartfelt interview on national television:

"I have a great attachment to Texas A&M," Bush said as he fought back tears. "I'm a little emotional, but the university will rally and recover. Right now, it's a time of chaos at the school, but things will be fine."

On campus, students walked to class like zombies, blank looks of sorrow on their faces. At the Bonfire site, where the logs still lay crumpled, the fences that cordoned off the stack were covered with flowers, notes, wreaths, and other tokens of sympathy.

At the base of the mighty flagpole that soars above the main drive into campus, one Aggie left his most prized possession—the coveted senior ring. After other Aggies followed his lead, dozens of rings from all class years sat untouched for days.

Media reports continued for days and gave people from far and wide a glimpse of this unique university. Suddenly, Texas A&M was seen as more than just a football school with its own version of an ROTC program. It was finally exposed for its family atmosphere, its sense of loyalty, its tangible spirit.

"We talk quite frequently here in terms of the bond Aggies have for one another," A&M football coach R. C. Slocum said. "And it gets to be a company line, the kind of thing other people don't put a lot of stock in. But times like these show what we've been talking about all along. You can see it more dramatically right now, but it's always been there."

A Yell Practice for the Ages

As the process of healing began on the A&M campus, there was the notion that despite all that the victims, their families, and the university had been through, the scheduled November 26 football game with the Texas Longhorns should still take place.

There was talk about canceling the game, but in the end, both schools felt it would be one way to honor the deceased students and to bring some sense of normalcy, however tenuous, to everyone involved.

A&M players fought through their own emotions—linebacker Christian Rodriguez had been a friend of casualty Jerry Self—and went about the business of preparing for a college football game. It wasn't going to be easy and it wasn't going to be fun, but as they practiced, the Aggie football team tried to push through the pain.

In Austin on the week of the game, the Longhorns were supposed to hold their annual Hex Rally, a candlelight ceremony to put a hex on the Aggies. This year, however, the Aggies and Longhorns would gather on the UT campus united as one. Instead of the traditional red candles used for the hexing, white ones (the color the schools have in common) were lit instead. As the majestic UT Tower was darkened, bells

*The **night before** the football game with the Longhorns, 50,000 people surrounded the Bonfire site in a candlelight vigil. After the eerily quiet tribute, Aggies filed into Kyle Field for the most memorable yell practice in school history.*

A record crowd was on hand at Kyle Field to watch the emotionally charged game between the Aggies and Longhorns. Among those in attendance were former President George Bush and then Texas Governor George W. Bush.

rang out across the campus. The song echoing through the buildings was "The Spirit of Aggieland."

Back in College Station, Aggie fans and mourners gathered the night before the game for a candlelight vigil that encircled the accident site. Fifty thousand people showed up, including both the future and former presidents from the Bush family. Hardly anyone uttered a word as the candles flickered in the breeze. Then, in one glowing procession, the Aggies headed to Kyle Field for a modified yell practice. Once again, the proud and sorrowful Aggies were marching in behind the Band.

Inside the stadium, the Aggie football team waited in bleachers on the field, and again, candles lit up the stands. Bonfire Red Pots, along with some of the students who had been injured in the collapse, lined the track that circles the field. ESPNEWS carried the yell practice live across the country.

Head Yell Leader Jeff Bailey, a typical yes-sir, no-sir Aggie, was about to lead his toughest yell practice ever.

"We've got to remember what Bonfire stood for," Bailey said to the hushed crowd. "What makes it special are the Aggies standing around it. So, as we stand here tonight, I

hope we yell louder, sing louder, and hold each other stronger than we ever have before.

"This yell practice is not about forgetting anything. It will always be in our minds as long as the spirit lasts here at Texas A&M."

After Coach R. C. Slocum addressed the crowd, and "The Spirit of Aggieland" was sung for a second time, the yell practice ended on an uplifting note. The A&M players headed for the tunnel into the locker room. But just as quickly, a few players, and then the whole team, turned and ran toward the Red Pots and the surviving victims.

Players hugged the students, acknowledging it was those same Aggies who had always supported their team. The stadium choked up again. And the most emotional A&M-Texas football game in the state's history had yet to kick off.

Tears and Cheers for the Rivals

The morning of November 26, 1999—only eight days after 12 people had been killed in one of the worst accidents ever to befall an American university campus—broke crisply into brilliant sunshine. No one connected to either Texas A&M University or the University of Texas knew what to expect as football fans headed to Kyle Field.

It was obvious from the time the Corps of Cadets began their traditional march into the stadium that this would be an A&M-Texas game

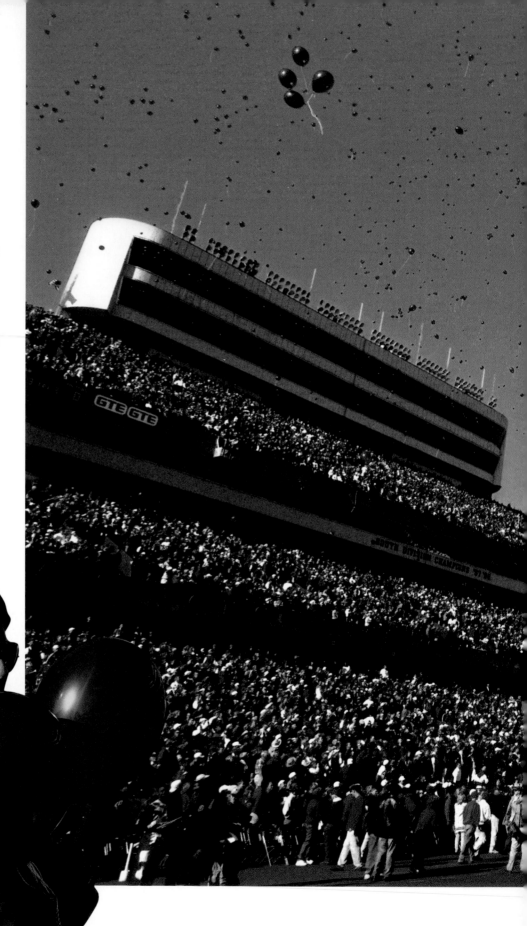

Before the game, maroon balloons and 12 white doves were released into the air. A jet fighter flyover (flown by A&M former students) roared across the blue sky as Aggies young and old honored the victims of the Bonfire collapse that had occurred just eight days earlier.

Aggie fans and Longhorn faithful were unsure how they would react once the November 26 game began. At halftime, both sets of fans would come together as one.

During a moment of silence just before kickoff, the only sound in the stadium was the flapping of 55 flags atop Kyle Field.

the likes of which would never be seen again. A riderless horse walked slowly around the perimeter of the field, and 12 white doves were released just before the flyover of F-16 fighter jets (all flown by former A&M students) in the "missing man" formation—one jet leaving the others and soaring straight up to the heavens. Fans of both schools wore maroon-and-white ribbons, while over 50,000 "Maroon Out" T-shirts had been sold. In an eerie coincidence, the number 12—a reference to the Aggies' 12th Man tradition—adorned the back of each shirt.

During a moment of silence just before kickoff, the only sound in the stadium was the flapping of 55 flags atop Kyle Field. Those high-flying flags honor Aggies who lost their lives in World War I. Now there was more remembrance, but for a tragedy that, unbelievably, had unfolded just across the campus.

Having been blown out by other Big 12–ranked teams like Oklahoma (51–6) and Nebraska (37–0), the 7–3 Aggies were underdogs to the 9–2, fifth-ranked Longhorns. The Horns, meanwhile, were on a roll, having won five straight games, including the 58–7 destruction of Texas Tech only a week before.

Texas players had begun the day on a sour note when nobody from the Ramada Inn had shown up to cook the team's breakfast—so

The Last Corps Trip

It was Judgment Day in Aggieland
And tenseness filled the air;
All knew there was a trip at hand,
But not a soul knew where.

Assembled on the drill field
Was the world-renowned Twelfth Man,
The entire fighting Aggie team
And the famous Aggie Band.

And out in front with Royal Guard
The reviewing party stood;
St. Peter and his angel staff
Were choosing bad from good.

First he surveyed the Aggie team
And in terms of an angel swore,
"By Jove, I do believe I've seen
This gallant group before.

"I've seen them play since way back when,
And they've always had the grit;
I've seen 'em lose and I've seen 'em win
But I've never seen 'em quit.

"No need for us to tarry here
Deciding upon their fates;
'Tis plain as the halo on my head
That they've opened Heaven's gates."

And when the Twelfth Man heard this,
They let out a mighty yell
That echoed clear to Heaven
And shook the gates of Hell.

"And what group is this upon the side,"
St. Peter asked his aide,
"That swelled as if to burst with pride
When we our judgment made?"

"Why, sir, that's the Cadet Corps
That's known both far and wide
For backing up their fighting team
Whether they won lost or tied."

"Well, then," said St. Peter,
"It's very plain to me
That within the realms of Heaven
They should spend eternity.

"And have the Texas Aggie Band
At once commence to play
For their fates too we must decide
Upon this crucial day."

And the drum major so hearing
Slowly raised his hand
And said, "Boys, let's play The Spirit
For the last time in Aggieland."

And the band poured forth the anthem,
In notes both bright and clear
And ten thousand Aggie voices
Sang the song they hold so dear.

And when the band had finished,
St. Peter wiped his eyes
And said, "It's not so hard to see
They're meant for Paradise."

And the colonel of the Cadet Corps said
As he stiffly took his stand,
"It's just another Corps Trip, boys,
We'll march in behind the band."

—by P. H. DuVal, Jr. (class of '51)

143

The Longhorn Band hoisted Texas A&M flags after playing moving renditions of taps and "Amazing Grace."

they had to resort to cereal without milk and Jack in the Box breakfast burritos as their pregame fare. But the Horns had to deal with more than just a light breakfast when they arrived at Kyle Field. Texas A&M, its football team, and its devastated fans were ready to come together in an almost spiritual commune to will the Aggies to victory.

As strong as that will was, A&M had to dig for every point in this extremely difficult game. In fact, Texas bolted to a 16–6 lead at halftime, and the already long faces at Kyle Field were sinking even more.

It was then that the crowd of 86,128 (a record for both Kyle Field and the state) was treated to perhaps the most heartfelt and poignant halftime show in both schools' history.

First to take the field was the "Showband of the Southwest," the Texas marching band. After playing taps and "Amazing Grace," the Longhorn band lowered its traditional Longhorn flags and simultaneously raised maroon flags to honor the Aggies. The band members then removed their white cowboy hats and left the field in silence.

As tears began to flow in the stands, it was the Aggie Band's turn to honor the fallen. Each football Saturday, all of Kyle Field—including visiting fans—waits with bated breath for the performance of the nationally famous Fightin' Texas Aggie Band. But today's performance would not be about precision turns and twists.

After playing its signature march "The Noble Men of Kyle," the Band formed its traditional, performance-ending block T. But silence—not the usual "Aggie War Hymn"—would provide the backdrop. As the Band marched off the field, only the jingle of spurs on the senior boots and the flapping flags above could be heard.

For the Aggies, the tears were about to turn to cheers. As A&M charged back into the football game, Kyle Field began to reverberate. When Ja'Mar Toombs sprinted around the corner for a nine-yard touchdown run with 4:47 left in the third quarter, cutting Texas's lead to 16–13, there was a sense that the Aggies could win this game.

That feeling heightened when, with neither team able to move the ball consistently in the fourth quarter, the Aggies finally pushed ahead (the Horns managed only 89 total yards and four first downs in the second half). After taking over on the UT 48-yard line and moving to the 14-yard line, A&M quarterback Randy McCown received the play from the sideline. He was to arch a fade pass into the corner of the end zone to his roommate, fellow senior Matt Bumgardner.

With 5:02 left in the game, McCown (who had completed just seven passes all game long) fired a perfect, lofting pass to Bumgardner, who positioned himself for the game-winning score. As he soared into the air and came down with the jump ball in the end zone, Kyle Field came unglued as the Aggies took a 20–16 lead.

But Longhorn quarterback Major Applewhite, the gutsy field general who had a stomach virus and did not play until the fourth quarter, had the stuff to keep the game in doubt. He drove the Horns to the A&M 45-yard line with under 30 seconds remaining. A long touchdown pass attempt was still in the works—but when Applewhite dropped back, A&M cornerback Jay Brooks pinched in on a blitz, popping Applewhite just as he was about to let go of the ball. Applewhite fumbled, and A&M linebacker Brian Gamble wriggled the ball away for the game-clinching fumble recovery.

Gamble looked skyward and raised his arms, honoring the Bonfire 12 as best he could. As the final seconds ticked off the clock, A&M linebacker Jason Glenn bent over and patted the maroon-and-white ribbon that had been stenciled into the Kyle Field grass. "It's over now," Glenn said. "It's all over."

Inside the Aggie locker room, hugs, high fives, and tears filled the room as the "Aggie War Hymn" bounced off the walls. After the celebration, several red-eyed Aggie players addressed an overflowing media press conference (712 media credentials were issued for the game, an A&M home-game record).

Offensive lineman Chris Valletta sat down before the throng of microphones wearing a sweat-soaked T-shirt bearing the names of the fallen Aggies. He shook his head in amazement when describing the

As the final seconds ticked off the clock, A&M linebacker Jason Glenn bent over and patted the maroon-and-white ribbon that had been stenciled into the Kyle Field grass. "It's over now," Glenn said. "It's all over."

145

The two schools will forever be linked to that special football game in 1999. On one emotional but glorious day, the state of Texas and its two flagship universities came together as never before.

scene they had just experienced. Another player, Brian Gamble, said, "We put our hearts and soul into this game. I know God and those Aggies were looking down on us. It was unbelievable."

As Aggie players began to file out of the locker room to be reunited with friends and family members, fans waited patiently for a glimpse of their heroes. But this game meant more than the usual Saturday cheers and applause. One elderly woman couldn't resist offering one more salutation. She approached the players and summed up Aggieland's indebtedness:

"I just wanted to thank you," she said tearfully. "Everyone in this community, everyone connected to this university, needed this."

Texas A&M would finish the season with an 8–4 record after a 24–0 loss to Penn State in the Alamo Bowl. Texas would end the year with a 9–3 mark following a 27–6 loss to Arkansas in the Cotton Bowl. But the two schools will forever be linked to that special football game in 1999. On one emotional but glorious day, the state of Texas and its two flagship universities came together as never before.

The Future of Bonfire

In the months following the Bonfire collapse, a Bonfire Commission was formed with outside engineers and consultants instructed to take an unbiased, in-depth look into both the stack's collapse and the culture of Texas A&M University. Leo Linbeck, Jr., the respected head of a large Houston construction company that specializes in the building of massive projects including skyscrapers and airports, was appointed to head the commission.

What the Bonfire Commission found in its extensive research and rounds of interviews were engineering, safety, and supervision flaws that came together to cause a horrific accident. The summary of findings disclosed in the May 2, 2000 final report reads as follows:

"The 1999 Bonfire collapsed due to a number of both physical and organizational factors. Structurally, the collapse was driven by a containment failure in the first stack of logs. Two primary factors caused this failure: the first was excessive internal stresses driven primarily by aggressive wedging of second stack logs into the first stack. The second was inadequate containment strength. The wiring used to tie the logs together provided insufficient binding strength. Also, steel cables, which in recent years had been wrapped around the first stack, were not used in 1999, further reducing containment strength. These two factors—excessive internal stresses and weakened containment strength—combined to cause the collapse.

John Comstock: A Remarkable Bonfire Survivor

Twelve Aggies died when Aggie Bonfire collapsed in the early morning hours of November 18, 1999. Surgeons at the College Station Medical Center were ready to add a thirteenth name—John Comstock—to the casualty list when he arrived in critical condition following a seven-hour ordeal beneath the tons of logs that had come crashing down.

Comstock was the last Bonfire victim removed from the crumpled stack of wood, and after sustaining massive internal injuries and bleeding uncontrollably, the status of this Aggie student was grave at best. His left leg was amputated, and doctors were removing dead tissue at an alarming rate.

Comstock went through 40 units of blood in one night, contracted jaundice from a split liver, and developed pneumonia from blood-filled lungs.

"The Monday night after the collapse was critical," said Dixie Edwards, Comstock's mother. "That's the night I went home, took a shower, put on clean clothes, and laid in the bed and waited for the phone call. We thought he would be dead by Tuesday morning."

But Comstock hung on, spending 83 days in the intensive care unit. During his hospital stay, Aggies kept a constant vigil on Comstock, with students often sleeping in the halls of the hospital near John's room. Over 50,000 cards from well-wishers poured in from all over the country, and "Pray for John" Web sites popped up on the Internet.

Comstock, who had fallen some 60 feet in the collapse, returned to his hometown of Dallas for rehabilitation that would last months. He arrived at the Zale Lipshy University Hospital weighing just 98 pounds, and his road to recovery was a bumpy one. Slowly—inch by inch—nerves began to grow back in his arms and legs, and by April 14, 2000,

Comstock was thrilled to be able to leave the hospital and return to his mother's home in the Dallas area.

By the fall of 2000, Comstock was going back to football games at Texas A&M. He had full range of motion in his arms, and moved around campus in a wheelchair.

Comstock re-enrolled at A&M as a junior in the fall of 2001. And despite some medical setbacks with kidney stones and pancreatitis, he was again back in his familiar Moses Hall, trying to enjoy Aggieland.

Comstock harbors no ill will toward A&M or Aggie Bonfire. In fact, if there had been another Bonfire to work on in the future, Comstock said he would be willing to help.

"Five years from now," Comstock says, "November eighteenth of '99 will be a day I wouldn't trade or wouldn't change to be where I am now, considering all the people I've met."

On November 18, 2000—
a year after the Bonfire collapse—
a memorial was held in the midst
of a cold, late autumn rain.

"The physical failure and causal factors were driven by an organizational failure. This failure, which had its roots in decisions and actions by both students and University officials over many years, created an environment in which a complex and dangerous structure was allowed to be built without adequate physical or engineering controls.

"This organizational failure is complex, but includes such things as the absence of an appropriate written design or design process, a cultural bias impeding risk identification, and the lack of a proactive risk management approach."

The Bonfire Commission had discovered the root of the problems associated with Bonfire. It was now up to president Ray Bowen to take the facts and assess them. Should he allow a scaled-back, safer Bonfire to be built under professional supervision in coming years? Or should he abolish the tradition altogether?

These were questions Bowen would have to deal with for the last two years of his presidency. On February 4, 2002, after consulting with hundreds of experts and student leaders, and after reviewing the almost 30,000 surveys that had been filled out by students and former students, Bowen came to the toughest decision he would make as a school administrator: Bonfire would not take place again.

Liability costs, safety concerns, and pending lawsuits all contributed to Bowen's decision. One insurance estimate, for $20 million worth of policies that would cover just one year of Bonfire construction, was over $475,000. The cost of materials and expert designs for a new Bonfire was estimated at $2.5 million; estimated costs for Bonfires thereafter were $1 million to $1.5 million each. In a time of budget shortfalls for higher education and out-of-control insurance costs, Texas A&M realized it was dealing with numbers that just didn't add up.

As time passed, Bowen claimed that the overwhelming response from Aggies everywhere assured him that he had made the right decision concerning Bonfire.

Plans for a permanent Bonfire Memorial were drawn up and were well received and approved by the A&M community. Bowen expressed hope that it would not be too long before A&M's energetic and enterprising students would soon begin a new, but safer, tradition, symbolic of that contagious and unique Aggie spirit—like the kind that began around a humble trash fire in 1909.

> **Sounding Off**
>
> "I've often heard that it is not the construction of the stack that made Bonfire important. It was asserted that it was important because of the fellowship and camaraderie that came from thousands of students working in unison on a challenging project.
>
> "My advice, for whatever the advice of a lame duck president is worth, is that the students face the inevitable and focus their energy on creating a new challenge, a new tradition. I believe that with a little effort another tradition can be created— one that has the benefits of Bonfire but does not carry the danger, on the one hand, or the expense, on the other. In my remaining years at A&M, as a faculty member, I hope to see a new tradition take root."
>
> —*Dr. Ray Bowen, president of Texas A&M University (February 4, 2002)*

THEY WILL REMAIN WITH US FOREVER
IN AGGIE SPIRIT

GAME DAY IN AGGIELAND

At Texas A&M, the game-day experience is a 24-hour expression of involvement, of loyalty, of showing off one of the most spirited places in the country.

AS MUCH AS THE PHYSICAL NATURE OF TEXAS A&M has changed over the decades—more students, more women, more buildings, and more traffic—it's the constants of the Aggie culture that keep Aggieland unique and beckon to its ever blossoming fan base.

Most students now walk to class dressed casually (flip-flops and T-shirts are more the norm than spit-shined shoes and pressed khaki), and the days when the A&W burger joint and Holick's were the hubs of off-campus activity are long gone.

In the fall, however, A&M returns to its roots. It is football season, after all, and the traditions so often associated with the school come out like the red sweaters at Nebraska and the bratwurst at Wisconsin.

For older Aggies especially, home football games represent six homecomings (seven, in some years), where they can hear the same songs, wear the same maroon polyester. They also feel the same chill down the spine that was part of the A&M experience back when John Kimbrough, John David Crow, or Johnny Holland were building their legends on the football field.

College football programs of all sorts profess to have one-of-a-kind autumn gatherings, which is why the sport has such a loyal following. Indeed, Saturdays spent along the river outside Tennessee's Neyland Stadium or inside The Grove at Ole Miss are can't-miss rites of revelry. But at Texas A&M, the game-day experience is characterized by more than just cold beer and hot brisket. It is a 24-hour expression of involvement, of loyalty, and of showing off one of the most spirited universities in the country.

Just as important, game day in Aggieland begins much earlier than on any other college campus: a hair past midnight, to be exact.

More Than a Pep Rally

Notre Dame can pack 10,000 fans into its Convocation Center on Friday nights for a pep rally, and the Fighting Irish's Friday afternoon luncheons with the head coach are legendary—

rubber-chicken affairs that draw 1,500 adoring fans. But only Texas A&M can fill up half a stadium for a yell practice at midnight before a home game. And that's what happens every time, no matter whether the Aggie football team has a date with a powerhouse or a pushover.

Yell practices began in 1913 as an occasional outlet for Cadets looking for a little diversion after dinner. But it wasn't until 1931 that the spirited rally that would become Midnight Yell Practice was held. That year, some Cadets who were gathered in Peanut Owens's dorm room in Puryear Hall decided to put some freshmen to work. The freshmen's task was to head across the street to the steps of the YMCA building to hold a yell practice at midnight. With the Texas game on the horizon and with the approval of senior Yell Leaders "Horsefly" Berryhill and "Two Gun" Herman, the Aggies began to gather around the building to practice a few yells in anticipation of the big game.

Today, Midnight Yell Practice is as much a part of the Friday night social scene in College Station as the crawfish boils that anchor Saturday night tailgate parties at LSU.

Aggie juniors, who guard Kyle Field during Midnight Yell Practice, are followed by Yell Leaders carrying torches at the start of a 1980s practice.

153

The Aggie Yell Leaders

Bill Youngkin, a Texas A&M Yell Leader in 1968 and 1969, jokes with newly elected Yell Leaders about their impending social life as the most visible and envied student leaders on campus: "If you have a girlfriend," Youngkin says, "get rid of her. You'll never be this cute and popular in your life."

Indeed, the experience of being a Texas Aggie Yell Leader is a special one, from the day you're elected by the student body to long after you've graduated.

While other schools have their pom-pom girls, gymnastic dynamos, and flashy dance teams prancing around on the sidelines, Texas A&M is known for its men in white. Dressed in the same outfits Yell Leaders wore a generation ago, five men (three seniors and two juniors, most of whom are in the Corps) lead the crowd in some of the same yells Aggies barked out at the turn of the 20th century.

Other cheerleading troupes use megaphones or microphones to try to drum up vocal support. In Aggieland, Yell Leaders use hand signals, which are passed up through the rows of seats to the top of the stadium, to indicate which of the five or six yells the student body will join in on. After counting to three with hand gestures, the Yell Leaders spin, gyrate, and flail their arms—all to the surprise of outsiders but to the comfort of the Aggies inside Kyle Field. Nearly 30,000 A&M students, who pack the east side of Kyle Field, have learned the yells—either during the summer through a traditions orientation called Fish Camp or by attending sporting events on the campus.

Witnessing the entire side of a stadium spell out A-G-G-I-E-S in unison can be overwhelming to opposing teams and an absolute rush for the five men lucky enough to be at the center of it all.

David Lawhorne, a senior Yell Leader in 1985, recalls the reaction of opposing cheerleading units when the Aggies would hit the road. A group of a few thousand Aggie fans was usually drowning out a far larger crowd of home fans. That's partly because the students bend over at the waist with their hands on their knees to perform the yells—in Aggie lingo, it's called humping it, which helps to draw as much noise as possible from each throat and set of lungs.

"I remember being at Alabama in 1985, and a couple of cheerleaders asked me how we got our fans to do that," said Lawhorne, the 2002 president of the Dallas A&M Club, one of the 179 A&M booster clubs throughout the world. "The yells are so sharp and so clear when you're on the field. They were amazed."

Yell Leaders are more than just orchestra conductors at football games. They spend the entire school year representing A&M at various booster functions and student gatherings. And the responsibility of carrying on the A&M tradition is taken seriously by the 200-plus living Yell Leaders.

"It's an honor, a privilege, and you're so proud to be a part of it," added Lawhorne. "You're bound by tradition to live up to the people who came before you. It's almost like you're a Yell Leader for life. At the mall or someplace, I still get pulled off to the side by people

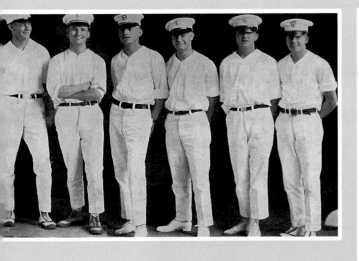

Yell Leaders still wear white as they did in 1919 (above). Today, the Yell Leaders direct the crowd at football games and yell practices, as well as serve as ambassadors for the school at various functions across the state of Texas.

who recognize me as a Yell Leader. We try to behave in a manner that would make the school proud of how we've lived our lives."

Youngkin, an attorney in Bryan–College Station, is one of a long line of Yell Leaders who have gone on to build successful careers and family lives. Rick Perry, a 1972 graduate of A&M and the governor of Texas after George Bush resigned to begin his presidential campaign, is also one of the prominent members of the Yell Leader family.

"It's a unique organization," a proud Youngkin says of the Former Yell Leaders Association. "I will be the Head Yell Leader of my class for the rest of my life."

The five male Yell Leaders (three seniors and two juniors) tote torches and march through campus with the Aggie Band, leading a procession of Corps members and on-campus residents into Kyle Field just before midnight. Awaiting them are the off-campus students and fans of A&M football who have already flooded into the stadium. For big games, close to 40,000 people gather for the traditional A&M yells, school songs, and fables read by the Head Yell Leader. Toward the end of the hour-long practice, the lights of Kyle Field are shut off and couples are given the opportunity to kiss under the stars. Fans without dates can flick a cigarette lighter so that—as the legend goes—they won't be dateless anymore.

The Aggies hold Midnight Yell Practice on the road as well, sometimes securing the host city's downtown landmarks as the site for their spirited sessions. Much to the locals' surprise, a yell practice can fill the streets, attracting crowds of curious onlookers. When the Texas game is in Austin, A&M fans flock to the steps of the state capitol, where Longhorn fans wait for a late-night clash before the big one on the field the following day.

A budding A&M fan watches as the Corps of Cadets begin their March-In to Kyle Field. The Corps marches into the stadium behind the Band, arriving 90 minutes before kickoff.

On six Saturdays in the fall (seven some years), the Aggie Corps of Cadets and famous Aggie Band are able to strut their stuff for all the world to see and hear.

The Aggie Band, which draws rousing ovations both at home and on the road, is the largest military marching band in the world. Lt. Col. Ray E. Toler (below) was only the fourth Aggie Band director in the long and storied history of the Band. Toler retired from his post in 2002.

Corps and Band on Parade

Much of what goes on inside the red brick walls of the Corps dorms on the A&M campus is kept in-house. It's a world of unseen discipline, secret terminology, and tributes to a traditional past. But on fall Saturdays, the Aggie Corps of Cadets and the Aggie Band strut their stuff for all the world to see.

The Corps March-In is one of the game-day highlights in Aggieland. Anticipation builds for hours along Joe Routt Boulevard, which leads out of the Quad, past Rudder Tower and the Memorial Student Center to the north end of Kyle Field. Under a canopy of aging oaks, thousands of Aggie fans—and a good turnout of visiting fans as well—line both sides of the street and straddle the center medians.

Kyle Field's capacity has been increased to 82,600, over 30,000 more than the 1975 capacity.

Ninety minutes before kickoff, a flurry of activity unfolds in the Quad (the falling out space between the Corps dorms), as friends, family members, and fans try to sneak an up close look at the Corps members' preparation. Pride swells on both sides of the family.

As the boom of a World War I howitzer echoes through the campus, the Aggie Band begins its march toward Kyle Field, with the entire Corps of Cadets and mascot Reveille falling in step right behind. The familiar military drumbeats pound down the pavement and straight through the hearts of Aggies young and old. As the Band cuts through the sea of maroon, the Corps members sound off with their familiar yells, exhibiting a true esprit de corps.

Once inside the stadium, the entire Corps marches around the field in formation as dignitaries and A&M officials look on from a reviewing stand. All the while, the two football teams warm up on the field and fans fill the stands.

Now is when the opposing players, cheerleaders, and visiting fans start surveying the scene with quizzical looks. The reaction is almost always the same: What have we gotten ourselves into?

Coming to a Crescendo at Kyle

Kyle Field is one of the largest and most intimidating college football arenas in the country. The nonstop energy and noise the field creates have been matched by few—if any—college football stadiums.

The fans who fill Florida's Ben Hill-Griffin Stadium (affectionately known as The Swamp), LSU's Tiger Stadium, and Tennessee's Neyland Stadium are among the most energetic in all of sports. And while all three can induce earsplitting noise for opponents, the level usually depends on the type of opponent and caliber of play on the field.

At A&M, the students stand for every game, for every opponent, for every situation. And the five Yell Leaders take their titles seriously. The program begins with the pregame singing of the school's alma mater, "The Spirit of Aggieland." As the entire stadium reverberates with words celebrating the spirit that "can ne'er be told," the Yell Leaders use their signature hand gestures to work the crowd into a concert of whooping and hollering that has echoed through the generations.

Five or six standard yells are used primarily for football games. And while some of the gestures the Yell Leaders use to lead the crowd may have changed over the decades, the effect of the routines never has: Aggie fans have a major impact on the football game.

Kyle Field generates more noise than most other stadiums because there are so many students, there's a higher proportion of students to older alumni, and the students stand throughout the game in honor of the 12th Man tradition.

While most schools might have as many as 10,000 students attend games, A&M reserves almost half the stadium for its student body. About two thirds of A&M students attend games each season, according to ticket officials, meaning that around 30,000 are present for each one. (By comparison, UT students enter lotteries for tickets for big games, and only about one fifth regularly attend.)

For big home games, such as the biennial affair with Texas or against one of the top-ranked Big 12 teams, Kyle Field transforms itself into a rollicking concert of towel-waving, throat-straining, vertigo-inducing zaniness. The crowd sways, and the stadium decks shimmy as Aggies lock arm in arm during the singing of the "Aggie War Hymn."

Matt Davison, a standout receiver for the Nebraska Cornhuskers from 1997–2000, describes the boisterous singing of the hymn during the 1998 A&M-NU game at Kyle Field as one of his most memorable college football experiences. "I remember looking up in the stands and getting queasy watching the fans going back and forth," Davison said with a laugh. "They really

At A&M, the students stand for every game, for every opponent, for every situation.

Did You Know?

There was an original 12th Man, and his name was E. King Gill. Gill had played on the A&M football team but switched to basketball, where he became a star. In 1922, he was attending the Dixie Classic in Dallas, acting as a spotter in the press box for *Waco News-Tribune* sports editor Jinx Tucker (the Dixie Classic was the predecessor to the Cotton Bowl). A banged-up A&M team was playing Centre College, and the number of Aggie injuries was mounting.

As the situation grew more dire, A&M coach Dana X. Bible called Gill down from the press box and told him to change into a football uniform—just in case. Under the grandstands (there was no real locker room in those days) Gill switched clothes with one of the injured Aggies and stood ready to help his school in any way he could.

Bible never had to put Gill into the game, and the Aggies went on to notch a 22–14 victory. But Gill had stood ready as the Aggies' "12th Man." The spirit and loyalty he showed was transformed into one of A&M's most storied and cherished traditions—one that has bound the Aggie student body together to this day.

Aside from the three drum majors, the members of the senior Bugle Rank hold the most prestigious spots in the Aggie Band.

support football. Everyone knows Nebraska has great fans, but for the Aggies, it's everything."

If the singing and swaying at Kyle Field doesn't affect opponents, the noise usually does. For the 2000 Oklahoma game, a noise meter was brought in to determine whether the din inside Kyle Field could set a decibel world record; it didn't, but it no doubt contributed to the fact that the Aggies nearly toppled eventual national champion OU.

While top-ranked Oklahoma survived the game 35–31, Kyle Field left a lasting impression on everyone lucky enough to have a ticket, just as it had in the 1998 Nebraska game, the 1989 Houston showdown, and the 1985 Texas clash. The same can be said of the visiting players fortunate enough to withstand the mayhem.

"Those 85,000 people standing the entire game, waving the 12th Man towels—it's unreal," said Kirk Herbstreit, on location at Kyle Field as an analyst for the popular ESPN road show, College Gameday. "Kyle Field and the 12th Man lived up to—and exceeded—every expectation we had for them. That Saturday in Aggieland provided, without a doubt, one of the most special memories I'll ever have from the show."

The Aggies Always Win Halftime

While fans at other schools may look on halftime as the 20-minute window for a bathroom break or an early start on postgame tailgating (fans at Oklahoma, for example, dash over to nearby O'Connell's for drinks), the halftime of an Aggie football game provides the chance to see one the most entertaining—and stunning—marching bands in the country.

The Fightin' Texas Aggie Band, with approximately 400 members, is the largest military-style marching band in the world. It first stepped off across campus in 1894 with just 14 members, coinciding with the first football season in Texas A&M history. Organized by bugler Joseph Holick (whose family has made the fabled senior boots in College Station for over 120 years), the early Aggie Bands merely provided cadence for the Cadets' marches to dinner and back— hardly the showstoppers that now receive standing ovations at every turn.

Even today, the Aggie Band's musicians are all members of the Corps of Cadets, and none attend A&M on music scholarships. Of the approximate 400 members, 90 were female in 2001–02. Using computer printouts to help design its intricate routines and practicing seven to 10 hours a week, the Aggie Band is

fronted by the prestigious three drum majors and a bugle line of 12 senior Cadets who lead the Band members down the football field or through downtown parade routes.

The Aggie Band is known for its stirring renditions of military marches and patriotic songs, and it has become so popular that Aggie fans yearn for the sounds of the "Pulse of the Spirit of Aggieland" for more than just a few fall Saturdays. In fact, a 1994 compact disk celebrating 100 years of the Aggie Band sold 100,000 copies, numbers that rank albums as platinum in the recording industry. A 30-minute television program, The Aggie Band Show, airs weekly in the fall in the Bryan–College Station market to give fans yet another dose of their beloved Band's unique talents.

Aggie Band halftime shows begin ceremoniously. As the Band forms at the north end of Kyle Field, the 80,000-plus fans rise to their feet with a hush. The head drum major barks out the standard com-

"Those 85,000 people standing the entire game, waving the 12th Man towels—it's unreal."

mands to begin the performance, which always starts with the "Aggie War Hymn," A&M's version of a fight song. With Aggies whooping in the stands, the senior boots who edge the formation step off in amazing unison.

Because the Aggie Band's drills can be so complex, the members are often seen turning their heads and instruments as they crisscross through lines of bandsmen. (If they didn't, it's anyone's guess how many would be popped by a wayward trombone!) After a 10 to 15 minute performance and another rousing ovation from the fans, the Band breaks ranks to run helter-skelter off the field. Another complicated—but usually flawless—routine has yet again wowed the crowd.

Circling Like Sharks

For all the noise the fans make, they won't let loose a sound that's heard regularly at other football venues across the country: the boo. Aggie fans never have— and never will—boo their own team, nor will they boo the opposing team.

Aggie fans are among the most knowledgeable and sophisticated football fans in the country, understanding the importance of good defense as much as the need to have a flashy quarterback under center. Because of A&M's long history of putting forth some of the nation's top defensive units (A&M finished first in total defense in 1975 and 1991), the Aggie crowd also knows well that fan noise can affect the rhythm of the opposition's offense. The second half of a football game has proved time and time again the powerful impact A&M fans can have. "We all have a stake in it," says Maj. Gen. Ted Hopgood, (Ret.). "It's like we're participants with what goes on at Kyle Field, not just spectators."

Former A&M defensive coordinator and former Notre Dame head coach Bob Davie used to refer to A&M fans as sharks on a feeding frenzy. Sensing the kill—not to mention that game-changing play—on third-and-long, the fans turn up the volume inside Kyle Field whenever the Aggie "Wrecking Crew" defense starts to circle around its prey.

At most stadiums, fans reach their loudest when a big touchdown is scored. At A&M, the fans rise up when they sense a quarterback sack is at hand.

But for all the noise the fans make, they won't let loose a sound that's heard regularly at other football venues across the country: the boo. Aggie fans never have— and never will—boo their own team, nor will they boo the opposing team.

"I think A&M fans have been the greatest of any school in the Big 12," said Max Urick, the athletic director at Kansas State University. "The demonstration of good sportsmanship is evident. I remember

Did You Know?

In 1986, the talkative Chet Brooks—a defensive back for the Aggies from 1984 to '87—decided the swarming and hard-hitting Aggie defense needed a nickname. Recounting the demolition and destruction that the Aggies had inflicted on opponents during the mid-1980s, Brooks dubbed the defense the Wrecking Crew. The nickname stuck, and defensive players at A&M still wear workout shirts and hats with "The Crew" emblazoned in maroon.

The Aggie defense not only has its own distinctive and famous nickname (perhaps only Nebraska's Black Shirt defense comes close in name recognition) but it has a new Aggie chant with its own hand signal: The index finger and thumb form a C and the three remaining fingers form W. It's already a student staple for big defensive stands.

our first visit to Texas A&M in 1996, and it was remarkable. Aggies spend their energy supporting their team, not booing the other one. Texas A&M should be held up as an example."

By the end of every game, the Aggie faithful have done their part, and usually so has the Aggie football team. In fact, in the decade of the '90s, the Aggies rolled up an amazing 55–4–1 home record, the fourth-best mark in all of college football. From 1990 to 1995, the Aggies won 31 straight games at home, the fifth-best home winning streak in the NCAA since World War II. From 1996 to 2000, A&M amassed a 22-game home winning streak that was snapped with a 26–19 loss to Colorado, and in R. C. Slocum's first 12 seasons as head coach, the Aggies posted perfect home records seven times.

After the final seconds tick off following another victory at Kyle Field, the freshmen in the Corps, or Fish, chase down the five Yell Leaders and carry them across campus for one final set of yell practices. The site is the Fish Pond fountain on the north side of campus. Then it's back to the YMCA building—the very place where such game-day enthusiasm first rang out in the night.

Sounding Off

"The alumni and students at A&M, by nature, are more conservative than at most schools. The school is just united more than Texas. Texas has got all the fraternities and all these things going on. Football may be important to a percentage of the people, but to a lot of them, they could care less about sports."

—Doug Forshagen,
University of Texas graduate and former executive committee member of A&M's 12th Man Foundation

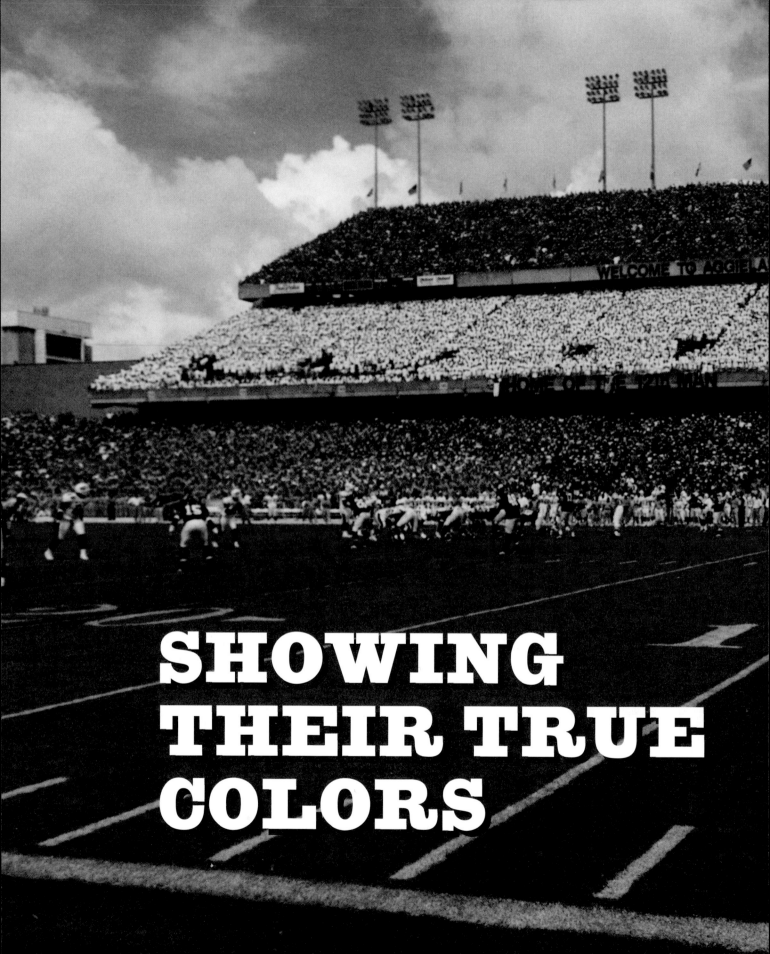

SHOWING THEIR TRUE COLORS

**The September 11 attacks jolted
Americans on a massive scale—
yet for Aggies everywhere,
that day of unspeakable horror
hit especially close to home.**

THE MORNING OF SEPTEMBER 11, 2001, dawned bright and clear in College Station, with a slight nip in the air that reaffirmed that, indeed, life was good in Aggieland. The oppressive Texas weather of late summer was turning ever so slightly, and football season was finally here in all its maroon splendor. Students emerged from the dorms and shuffled off to their 8 a.m. classes as the Texas A&M campus crackled to life again on a sparkling Tuesday morning.

But this would not be another routine September day at A&M—or anywhere else. Just before 9 a.m., the horror began with the terrorist attack on the twin towers of the World Trade Center, spread to the Pentagon and a Pennsylvania field, and escalated with the collapse of the towers into concrete dust and death. The world as anyone knew it would be scarred and changed forever.

At Texas A&M, a place as patriotic and spirited as any institution in the U.S.A., the dazed looks on the faces of students and faculty told an all too familiar story of unthinkable loss. The September 11 attacks jolted Americans on a massive scale—yet for Aggies everywhere, that day of unspeakable horror hit especially close to home. The kind of helplessness and grief felt by the A&M community in the moments after the 1999 Bonfire tragedy now enveloped a country that was having to come to terms with those unanswerable questions: How? Why? Where do we go from here?

As the nation slowly began to heal even as it prepared for war, heartfelt tributes to the heroes at ground zero and emotional salutes to the very fiber of freedom covered the United States like a warm blanket. Sporting events—especially football and postseason baseball games—became public displays of togetherness and steadfastness. They were memorial services held at altars and shrines that sat 75,000.

Texas A&M, having been through a communal calamity of its own two years earlier, was about to honor America and its heroes and victims as no other school could. Thanks to some enterprising A&M students—plus former students following their lead—the Aggies pulled off one of the most amazing 10 days of cooperation and coordination imaginable.

The spectacular result was a football stadium decked out in red, white, and blue cotton T-shirts and, later, the delivery of almost $200,000 to New York City police and firemen. To those watching from afar, it was a stunning exhibition of patriotism and love of country. To the Aggies, it was just another chance to stand up for America and to give something back.

Once the students shoehorned *themselves into the east side stands, it was obvious that Kyle Field was turning into a red, white, and blue spectacle that could only have unfolded in Aggieland.*

The Impact of the Internet

Just a day after the September 11 attacks, Texas A&M junior Eric Bethea decided to visit the Aggie sports Web site known as Texags.com, one of the most widely used independent college athletic Web sites in the country. Although Texags.com was welcoming its usual number of Aggie diehards to its message forums, the discussion didn't center on football recruiting, the merits of a particular player, or the lack of diversity in the A&M offense.

Rather, on this day of mourning, Aggies were sending messages of comfort to one another. Just as it had in the somber days following the Bonfire tragedy of '99, Texags.com had become one big therapy session on the information superhighway.

Inspired by the outpouring of support, Bethea had an idea to rally the Aggies on a massive scale and pay tribute to America in a manner that was not only grand but gripping. He called for a "Red, White, and Blue Out" game at Kyle Field.

In the summer of 1998, "Maroon Out" had become Aggieland's newest tradition, unveiled for the coming showdown with No. 2 Nebraska at Kyle Field. The aptly named Kyle Valentine, an enterprising Aggie student, had proposed to the student body and former students that everyone wear a maroon shirt. This would turn the east side of Kyle Field into a sea of maroon, one-upping Nebraska's tradition of painting the stadium in its primary school color—bright red.

Valentine organized a student committee to sell maroon T-shirts at $5 apiece on the Internet and various points on the A&M campus. After the university granted approval to sell the shirts around Kyle Field on game days, Valentine's idea took off, and over 50,000 specially designed Maroon Out shirts were sold by the Nebraska game's kickoff. In a remarkable scene, the entire east side of Kyle Field—the student side—was awash in maroon. Aggie ingenuity had paid off again with another proud exhibition of school spirit.

Valentine and his workers had been allowed to market the Maroon Out T-shirts for months before the October 10 game with the Cornhuskers. But Eric Bethea had just over a week to implement his patriotic plan before the September 22 home game with Oklahoma State—and it wouldn't be easy. For one thing, the novelty of Maroon Out had worn off just a bit as the years passed. For another, detractors of Bethea's plan claimed that no color coordination this ambitious could be orchestrated in such a short

Did You Know?

The Maroon Out tradition, started in 1998 for the Nebraska game, involves Texas A&M students wearing an officially designed maroon T-shirt for the designated Maroon Out game each year. But the tradition became so popular that almost all students at games are now wearing maroon T-shirts. In the past, white T-shirts were customarily worn because of the hot and humid conditions in September and October.

amount of time, especially during an unsettled time of anger and grief.

Still, Bethea's idea began to gain support as he proposed to outfit Kyle Field's three decks in the colors of the American flag. Luckily, the north end zone of Kyle Field, expanded with a club and suite level in 1999, had a three-deck configuration that was made to order for Bethea's color scheme of red, white, and blue.

While the plan had both moxie and merit, Bethea needed thousands of T-shirts. More important, he needed the cooperation of the fans. And the clock was ticking.

The Call Goes Out

The Aggies' football schedule actually worked in favor for the overwhelming task these Aggie students were about to take on. The schedulemakers had given A&M an idle Saturday on September 15 (although it turned out that all college and professional games would be canceled that week), and the next scheduled game was at home with the Big 12 opener against Oklahoma State. Had the Aggies been scheduled to hit the road on September 22, the dazzling effect of the planned display could have lost some of its poignancy.

Luck may have been on their side in that respect, but the five primary organizers of Red, White, and Blue Out—Eric Bethea, Cole Robertson, Nick Luton, Josh Rosinski, and Kourtney Rogers—were still faced with calling on every available student helper, T-shirt vendor, and media machine they could find to spread the word.

The first organizational meeting for the event began inauspiciously, to say the least. On a Sunday afternoon, just six days before the Oklahoma State game, the organizers called on students to discuss logistics for pulling off this special tribute. But the volunteers who showed up were few and far between. Just as quickly as Bethea's idea had been hatched, the possibility of pulling off the Red, White, and Blue Out spectacle began to wane.

Yet the leaders pressed on, contacting the owner of a College Station T-shirt printing shop. Bethea thought the students should order 7,000 shirts to start, while Nick Luton pushed that number to 10,000. Ken Lawson, the president of the accommodating printing shop, C. C. Creations, thought in even bigger terms, convinced that the idea would take off. The first order of shirts topped out at 15,000—enough to cover the backs of half the students who would walk through the gates of Kyle Field, and an impressive feat in itself.

With peer pressure mounting inside the A&M walls to back this spirited endeavor (and with the aid of cell phones and the Net), news of the event was spreading from the bank offices of Houston to the ranches of West Texas. The students of Texas A&M were up to their old tricks again, banding together to reach a common goal. Like earlier Aggies,

Just as quickly as Bethea's idea had been hatched, the possibility of pulling off the Red, White, and Blue Out spectacle began to wane.

who built Bonfires or gathered en masse at yell practices on the steps of the YMCA building, these modern day Aggies were the antithesis of the slacker generation.

On Monday morning, after students were told via the Internet which color shirt they should buy (those in the third deck, red; in the second, white; and in the first, blue), boxes of shirts arrived at the plaza that spreads out just outside the north end of Kyle Field. Seniors, who are allowed to pick up their tickets on the Monday of game weeks, were also given first choice of the $5 T-shirts. Because seniors at A&M pack the best deck for viewing on the east side of Kyle Field—the second— the white T-shirts sold out quickly on day one.

Juniors were next in line to grab tickets and shirts, and by 7 a.m. the following day, lines of hundreds of students snaked around the Kyle Field Plaza. But a problem loomed: Shirts were selling so briskly that sophomores and freshmen might not even have a chance to participate in the Red, White, and Blue Out.

Even though the workers at C. C. Creations were laboring in 24-hour shifts to print the T-shirts, time was running out. To make

On game day, fans began arriving on campus much earlier than usual. In fact, there was a flurry of activity at the T-shirt tables as early as 7 a.m.

the event work, the Aggie community—at least those who own T-shirt shops—would have to pitch in.

The Red, White, and Blue Out committee, which had blossomed to hordes of students, would now make this dream come true. They started by canvassing the Bryan–College Station area for T-shirt printers, enlisting them, and even helping to dry, fold, and box the shirts as they rolled off the presses. Soon, T-shirt vendors from all over Texas were offering their services. By the end of the week, with the demand for the shirts skyrocketing to unheard-of proportions, T-shirts were being printed in Dallas and Houston and driven by students in U-haul trucks back to College Station day and night.

By Friday of game week, it had become obvious that the original order for 15,000 red, white, or blue T-shirts—with the words Standing for America emblazoned across the front—had been astonishingly low. The Aggies—the kings of doing things in unison—would need almost five times that number.

Kyle Field Is All Decked Out

Texas A&M and Oklahoma State were set to kick off on September 22 at 11:30 a.m., which meant an early wake-up call for the thousands of Aggie fans pouring in from across the state of Texas. But because the fans were fully aware of the frenzy over Red, White, and Blue Out, the foot traffic on the Texas A&M campus even at 7 a.m. was startling. Lines of Aggie fans stretched longer and longer at the many T-shirt tables. Student workers were throwing shirts at buyers and stuffing thousands of dollars inside backpacks used as makeshift safes. Former students were so impressed by the students' efforts that many generous alumni stuffed $100 bills into the overflowing coffers as tips.

Fans who hadn't learned beforehand of the Red, White, and Blue Out event were caught dumbfounded, scurrying for shirts to blend in with the rest of the crowd. Some fans—men and women alike—were changing shirts (discarding the coveted maroon) in plain view. Oklahoma State fans even joined in the patriotic rush, shedding their bright orange to join the Aggies' T-shirt brigade on this special day.

Before the gates of Kyle Field were opened, there was a sense that Red, White, and Blue Out was going to be a

Before the gates of Kyle Field were opened, there was a sense that Red, White, and Blue Out was indeed going to be a big success. But it wasn't until the fans and students flowed into Kyle Field to fill their designated red, white, or blue decks did the enormity of this tribute come into focus.

177

R. C. Slocum and the Texas A&M coaching staff added a nice touch by donning the official Red, White, and Blue Out T-shirts instead of their usual game-day garb. Even Reveille VI wore a corsage trimmed in the patriotic colors of America.

resounding success. But it wasn't until the fans and students flowed into Kyle Field to fill the designated decks that the enormity of this tribute came into focus.

As the late arriving students filed in, the sight of the east side of Kyle Field was astonishing. The entire top two decks—with just a sprinkling of uncoordinated shirts—were solid red above, white below. The first deck—with the Corps of Cadets dressed as usual—was a mixture of 80 percent blue and 20 percent khaki. To the surprise of most, former students and other fans of A&M had taken the students' lead and blanketed the west side and north end zone decks of Kyle Field in the appropriate colors as well. Kyle Field had turned into the nation's largest—and most stunning—display of the national colors.

Cole Robertson, a junior and one of five students who helped organize Red, White, and Blue Out, recalls being overwhelmed when he first walked into Kyle Field on September 22: "The emotions I experienced were incredible. I was tearing up and choking up at the same time." Just nine days earlier, the idea of painting the stadium in America's colors had been a whim. Now, after sleepless nights and the confluence of spirit and cooperation from all over Texas, 70,000 fans were wearing red, white, and blue T-shirts in honor of the heroes and victims of one of the darkest days in American history.

As the A&M coaches—dressed in either red, white, or blue T-shirts instead of the usual Nike game-day garb—gathered the team in the locker room just before game time, R. C. Slocum spoke to his players about living up to the dedication and patriotism the A&M and OSU fans had already shown at this once-in-a-lifetime event. Listening to his coach, linebacker Christian Rodriguez wondered how a football game could dare match what had already been created in the

stands: "It was very emotional," Rodriguez said of the pregame meeting. "Sitting in the locker room before the game I was like, 'God, how am I to go out there and focus on the plays when I see all of that red, white, and blue?"

Once the game began, A&M and Oklahoma State battled to a 7–7 tie at halftime, and football again took center stage in Aggieland. But then came the 20 minutes of tribute the Aggie Band had perfected before. Just as in the 1999 Bonfire game against Texas, the Aggie Band was called on to march with equal parts precision and compassion.

Appropriately, the Corps of Cadets was celebrating the one-hundred-and-twenty-fifth year of its existence on the weekend of the Oklahoma State game. The Aggie Band spelled out "125" across the field to honor the anniversary, but the biggest chills for the crowd came as the Band formed the letters USA sideline to sideline as "God Bless America" blared from midfield.

> ### Did You Know?
> The 70,000 red, white, and blue T-shirts (the front of the shirts read, In Memory of 9-11-01, STANDING FOR AMERICA, Aggieland, USA, September 22, 2001) were sold in the space of a week, including 30,000 on game day alone. That's 16,000 more than the Maroon Out T-shirts sold for the 1998 Nebraska game at Kyle Field.

Sounding Off

"Everyone involved in football saw Red, White, and Blue Out and saw it for what it was: A spectacular display of patriotism that was all designed and operated by students. You can't describe what it was like to come out and see that stadium, because no one had ever seen anything like it. Patriotism and devotion to country are a part of A&M, and I'm very proud of that."

—*Texas A&M football coach R. C. Slocum*

The Aggie football team pulled away in the second half for a 21–7 victory over the Cowboys of Oklahoma State University, pushing their record to 3–0. The huge game with Notre Dame was next up on the docket, but as 82,601 fans filed out of Kyle Field, there was little eagerness for another football game a week later.

After all, the country and Texas A&M were still in mourning, even if a colorful and patriotic outpouring at a football game had eased the pain and pumped up the pride on another autumn afternoon in Aggieland, U.S.A.

The Aggies Head to New York City

Red, White, and Blue Out raised $180,000 in T-shirt sales, and its organizers were dead set on hand-delivering the money to the New York Fire Department and Police Department relief funds. But as college students in a tight economy, the fabulous five still needed a little help to make their dream of an East Coast trip a reality.

That's when the Aggie network—plus a number of gracious airline and hotel companies—reached out for the good of the cause. One longtime Aggie supporter, David Evans, had been overwhelmed when he walked into Kyle Field on September 22. He told his fellow members of the Baytown A&M Club that the students who worked so hard to turn Kyle Field into an unforgettable red-white-and-blue spectacle deserved some kind of major recognition.

Sending the organizers on a trip to New York seemed like the right thing to do. Evans first contacted Continental Airlines, which, after hearing of the project, quickly agreed to contribute round-trip tickets to the five Aggie students. A Hilton Hotel in New York City was so impressed with the Aggies' efforts that the chain chipped in five complimentary rooms. To top it off, after the New York City Police Department agreed to a proper donation ceremony, an anonymous A&M booster gave each of the students $200 in spending money. Said Evans, "It's phenomenal that in a matter of about nine days, five young people put something like that together and pulled it off. These kids really deserved the proper recognition for all they did."

While the five students were given a rousing send-off in College Station and rated front-page billing in the local newspaper, there was more to the trip than sightseeing and even presenting a pair of $90,000 checks to the police and fire departments of New York City. It was about a group of Aggies rallying together for one common goal: To help ease the pain of our nation's most devastating tragedy in over half a century.

The organizers of Red, White, and Blue Out presented $180,000 to the New York City police and fire relief funds—$90,000 each.

The five chief leaders of *Red, White, and Blue Out were first row, from left: Kourtney Rogers, Josh Rosinski, Nick Luton, Cole Robertson and back row, far right, Eric Bethea. Former student David Evans top, center, helped organize the New York City trip for the group.*

Back on the Texas A&M campus, the events of September 11, 2001, were as unforgettable to Aggies as they were to millions of Americans. True to their history, students and former students had found a way to bring themselves even closer together. From the Bonfire tributes in 1999 to the patriotic outpouring at Red, White, and Blue Out, Texas A&M continued to show its true colors in ways that few schools could ever imagine.

AGGIE TRADITIONS

The activities showcased at A&M football games tell only half the story. These and other traditions are grounded in the loyalty, camaraderie, respect, and goal-sharing that are a part of Aggie life seven days a week.

E VERY AUTUMN, THE SIGHTS, SOUNDS, AND SMELLS of college football play to the senses of millions of fans. The pageantry of the pregame ceremony, the bands of the halftime, and the postgame boasting and toasting are what stick in the minds of the college football faithful.

What's more, football seasons rarely change. Oh, sure, a different team may win the conference or national title every fall, and Football U. may have a season where the losses outnumber the wins. But the comforting sameness and traditions of college football keep us coming back for more.

Take the University of Michigan, for example. There, the legendary maize-and-blue helmets—designed to represent the old leathered look of the headgear of yesteryear—are classics, and as traditional as the sport they represent. At LSU, the Bayou Bengals wear their usual white jerseys at home and always take to the field by sprinting under the same crossbar of the same goalpost.

The Horns of Texas flash their "Hook 'em" sign with pinky and index fingers held high, and the Trojans of USC form a V for victory with theirs. Notre Dame's helmets sparkle as brightly as the Golden Dome and the mosaic of Touchdown Jesus that rise just outside the hallowed walls of Notre Dame Stadium. Washington and Washington State collide in the annual Apple Cup; rivals Purdue and Indiana vie for the Old Oaken Bucket; and Auburn and Alabama captivate the country each November in their nasty throwdown known as the Iron Bowl.

Then there's Texas A&M, which is known more for its traditions, perhaps, than for any of its other aspects. Yet the activities showcased at A&M football games—including the Aggie Band's halftime routine and the students' game-long standing in honor of the 12th Man legend—tell only half the story. These and other traditions are grounded in the loyalty, camaraderie, respect, and goal-sharing that are a part of Aggie life seven days a week.

While such noble characteristics gave birth to the traditions of Aggieland generations ago, few outside of A&M circles have ever actually seen these expressions of spirit up

Silver Taps is one of the most revered traditions on the Texas A&M campus. Once a month, if an A&M student has died during that period, fellow students gather outside the Academic Building to pay tribute to the fallen Aggie. With campus lights dimmed, a 21-gun salute is given, and buglers atop the building play taps.

close. More than just the rah-rah and sis-boom-bah of a football game, they exist as heartfelt tributes, from the monthly Silver Taps gatherings to the April 21 Muster ceremonies held around the world.

"Texas A&M's traditions are the shaft that holds the point of the sword," says A&M archivist David Chapman. "You're always looking at the point, but the shaft holds it all together."

Silver Taps

More than 44,000 students attend Texas A&M University, making it an on-campus city of activity each school day. But the hustle and bustle come to a halt in the evening on the first Tuesday of every month. In honor of any current A&M student who has died during that month, the touching tribute called Silver Taps is held at the front of the Academic Building. Campus flags are flown at half-mast throughout the day, and around 10 p.m., the lights of the campus are turned out.

As hundreds of students silently gather to honor the deceased—usually a stranger to most students, but an Aggie nonetheless—the elite Ross Volunteers of the Corps of Cadets (RVs) slowly march to the front of the Academic Building. The RVs, who also serve as the honor guard of the governor of Texas, fire three volleys into the night air as part of a 21-gun salute. Then, hidden atop the roof of the Academic Building, buglers from the Aggie Band play a moving rendition of taps.

As the ceremony ends and students shuffle back to their dorms, there's a sense amid the solemnity that the familiar campus slogan—"Once an Aggie, always an Aggie"—is more than just a catchy jingle.

191

Aggie Muster

While Silver Taps honors those students who have died during a particular month, Aggie Muster is an annual tribute to the deceased of the Aggie family. On one day, thousands gather all over the world to honor fallen Aggies, young and old. Held on April 21—the anniversary date of Gen. Sam Houston's victory in 1836 over Santa Anna's army at San Jacinto to gain Texas's independence from Mexico—Aggie Muster is perhaps A&M's most treasured tradition.

The event started on June 26, 1883 as an annual gathering of college buddies reliving the old days at the Agricultural and Mechanical College of Texas—little more than a typical college reunion. But by April 21, 1922, it had changed complexion, becoming an annual rite to pay tribute to those Aggies who were no longer with us.

One of the most significant Aggie Musters came in 1942, on the Philippine island of Corregidor. Under siege from the Japanese during World War II, Gen. George Moore, class of 1908, nevertheless convened with 24 other Aggies on the island for the April 21 tradition, aware that there was every possibility that the soldiers would be among those whose names were reverently called at Muster the next year.

Aggie Muster is held each April 21 in cities around the world, with the largest ceremony taking place on the main Texas A&M campus. Candles are lit to represent each Aggie who has died during that year.

Overleaf:
***The Ross Volunteers,** an elite unit of the Corps of Cadets, fire a 21-gun salute in honor of those Aggies who have passed on.*

Did You Know?

A&M freshmen are affectionately called Fish, and nearly 5,000 incoming students attend an optional summer orientation known as Fish Camp. Held at a Lutheran Church retreat in the thick woods near Palestine, Texas, the popular event is organized by 900 counselors (all upperclassmen) and is held over six sessions every August. At each one, Fish are taught the famous Aggie traditions and the intricacies of life on the A&M campus.

The largest Muster is held on the main Texas A&M campus, where a keynote speaker leads off the ceremony.

But it is the Muster Roll Call—when the names of the deceased Aggies are read and friends or family members answer "here"—that jerks at the heartstrings of those who attend. After each response, a candle is lit, ensuring that while those Aggies aren't present in body, they will forever live on in the Aggie spirit.

The Aggie Ring

You see them on shoppers at the grocery store. You've spotted them on tourists on the New York subway. And you're as likely to see one on the hand of a Dallas CEO as you are on a South Texas rancher. For Aggies, the Ring is definitely the thing.

The first Aggie Ring was designed for the class of 1889, and five years later senior E. C. Jonas came up with the version still worn today. The only significant change in the Aggie Ring's design came in 1963, when the Texas Legislature changed the university's name from the Agricultural and Mechanical College of Texas to Texas A&M University.

The Aggie Ring—ordered by an astonishing 85 percent of A&M undergraduates—is awarded to seniors who have passed over 95 credit hours. The numerals of the senior class year, placed just below a shield that symbolizes an Aggie's desire to protect the university, are the dominant feature on the ring face.

The ring face is worn inward until seniors graduate, at which point they turn their rings outward so that the class year will "face the world proudly, just as the Aggie graduate will be ready to face the world." For former A&M students, the Aggie Ring becomes an instantly recognizable connection to their university.

Each symbol on the Aggie Ring has been thought out, from the 13 stripes on the shield (representing the 13 original states of America)

Eighty-five percent of A&M undergraduate students order Aggie Rings. It is the largest order of school rings in the country.

to the crossed flags of the state of Texas and the U.S.A. (recognizing an Aggie's allegiance to both state and country).

Perhaps only the military academies cherish their class rings as much as seniors and graduates of Texas A&M University do. When the Aggie Bonfire collapsed in 1999, some of the most poignant pieces of remembrance were those Aggie Rings left at the base of the large flagpole that rises just above the Polo Fields where the tragedy

Before each home football game, *flowers are placed on the graves of each Reveille that has served A&M as its official mascot.*

As the Aggies' official mascot, this full-blood American collie prances across the Texas A&M campus as if she has no doubt that she is the highest-ranking member of the Corps of Cadets and the First Lady of Aggieland.

occurred. The gold Aggie Rings (priced from $286 to $539) remained untouched for days as the Aggie community grieved for the 12 students who died in the tragic accident.

A Mascot Named Reveille

From the sidelines of Kyle Field to the basketball baseline of Reed Arena, Reveille rules the roost. As the Aggies' official mascot, this full-blood American collie prances across the Texas A&M campus as if she has no doubt that she is the highest-ranking member of the Corps of Cadets and the First Lady of Aggieland.

And she has the pedigree to prove it. The Reveille tradition began in January 1931, when a group of cadets were traveling back to College Station. Their vehicle hit a small black-and-white dog, and the Aggies had no second thoughts about bringing her back to campus to nurse her wounds. The next morning, as the Corps of Cadets began to gather for morning drills and reveille blared from the bugle stand, the dog began to bark incessantly.

The Cadets named her Reveille, and the following football season—after Reveille led the Aggie Band onto the field for its halftime performance—she was

Reveille attends all A&M football games, both home and away. For longer trips, the well-treated mascot often flies on a private university plane.

declared A&M's official mascot. When Reveille I died in 1944, she was given a formal military funeral and buried outside the north end of Kyle Field, facing the scoreboard so that she—and all future Reveilles—could keep track of the Aggies' football exploits.

Before naming a second Reveille, the school tried out other unofficial monikers—Tripod, Spot, and Ranger—but decided to keep the Reveille name. Reveille VII, introduced as the latest Aggie mascot in April 2001, attends every class with her sophomore handler, a Mascot Corporal from Company E-2 of the Corps of Cadets. Like her predecessors, she sleeps in a dorm room—and, as the tradition goes, if she decides to occupy a bed, a Cadet is out of luck for a good night's sleep. Should the well-trained Reveille bark during a class, the professor is "urged" to dismiss class for the day.

Reveille VII may have been forced to attend obedience school, but at least she didn't have to suffer the early trauma that Reveille VI endured. Just before the 1994 Cotton Bowl in Dallas, Reveille VI (still a puppy) was staying with her handler's parents in a Dallas suburb for the holidays. But after casing the area, a group of conniving University of Texas students stole Reveille VI out of the backyard and then spirited her away to Austin.

Thankfully, the puppy was found two days later, tied to a post on an Austin street corner. That dognapping was the first time the Aggie mascot had ever been the victim of such college hijinks—but in keeping with her dedication to Texas A&M, Reveille VI was on the sidelines for the Aggies' Cotton Bowl matchup with Notre Dame.

The 12th Man

The 12th Man tradition at Texas A&M has become so synonymous with the university that the phrase is now copyrighted. Indeed, the term 12th Man has come to connote an almost mystical being that represents the ghosts of Aggies past.

It all started when basketball standout E. King Gill pledged his support to help an injury-riddled Aggie football team at the Dixie Classic in 1922. Gill never entered the game, but it was his willingness to stand ready—just in case—that came to symbolize the Aggies' undying devotion to one another and their school.

Since that memorable day in Dallas, the 12th Man has evolved into a catchphrase that describes the entire crowd of Aggies at Kyle Field. Huge maroon letters shouting "Welcome to Aggieland, Home of the 12th Man" are emblazoned across the façades of the decks on the east side of the stadium.

The 12th Man Kickoff Team of non-scholarship players began in 1983. It was created by coach Jackie Sherrill, who was inspired by the spirit of A&M students as they worked atop the stacks of Bonfire.

Sherrill had just arrived in College Station, some 60 years after E. King Gill attended school. Yet the characteristics that bound the Aggies together back in 1922 were still remarkably obvious.

In 1988, the 12th Man Foundation took the name knowing it would appeal to the generous legion of Aggies who always support the team—win or lose—financially. Raising funds for athletic scholarships and facility improvements since 1950 (it was known as the Aggie Club for almost 40 years), the 12th Man Foundation has become one of the nation's largest athletic fund-raisers.

In keeping with A&M's astonishing growth, the foundation has seen annual funds quadruple over the last 10 years. While the Aggies have won only four national championships—football in 1939 and softball in 1982, '83, and '87—membership in the 12th Man Foundation has grown fivefold, to over 24,000 donors.

Some outsiders claim that the many traditions and cultural quirks of Texas A&M give the school an almost cultist feel. If you're not already a part of the 12th Man, they wonder, can you ever be?

Dennis Mudd, one of the early members of the 12th Man Kickoff Team, speculates on the answer to that question: "There's a contagious spirit and loyalty that you get from this school," he says. "And it's passed on from family to family. Some people say we brainwash our kids. I say, 'No, we just take them to football games.'"

The statue of E. King Gill, the original 12th Man, is located just outside Kyle Field in the Zone Plaza.

The 12th Man has evolved into a catchphrase that describes the entire crowd of Aggies at Kyle Field. Huge maroon letters shouting "Welcome To Aggieland, Home of the 12th Man," are emblazoned across the façades of the decks on the east side of the stadium.

Epilogue
VISION FOR THE FUTURE

THE HISTORY OF TEXAS A&M UNIVERSITY has been an amazing one, from its early days as an all-male, military school to its current status as a major coeducational university on a sprawling megacampus.

Much has changed in Aggieland: The curriculum has been expanded, enrollment has soared, and A&M's academic reputation has improved to the point where the school is now considered one of the nation's most prestigious public universities.

And the school is aiming even higher. With its Vision 2020 initiative to improve all aspects of the university in place, Texas A&M seeks to join the elite as one of the top 10 public universities in the United States by the year 2020.

"The key to Vision 2020 is the challenge of improving the academic programs while preserving and strengthening the traditions, culture, and spirit of the university," says A&M president Dr. Robert Gates, who assumed the post in fall 2002.

The infrastructures of A&M and College Station have been overhauled through the generations, and Kyle Field nearly doubled in capacity over the course of 25 years. (The idea of a 100,000-seat football stadium within the next 10 years is a real possibility.) But what has kept A&M unique—and so special—has little to do with bricks and mortar. It has substantially more to do with the people and values that have shaped the university since its days as a tiny land-grant school in the flatlands of Brazos County.

Earning a degree from A&M is a multifaceted experience of growing together under an incredible umbrella of spirit, passion, and loyalty toward something grander than yourself. It all started with the Corps of Cadets over a century ago. Yet despite the astonishing growth of the school, the devastation of war, and the tragedy of the Bonfire collapse, Texas A&M's signature spirit has endured.

The makeup of the student body may have changed dramatically over the years, but 30,000 students still fill half a football stadium on game days. Five thousand incoming freshmen still descend into the Piney Woods of Texas every August to orient themselves with the "spirit that can ne'er be told." People still greet each other with a friendly "Howdy" on cam-

PLAY LIKE CHAMPIONS TODAY

pus, and respond with a "Here" when roll call is read at Aggie Muster.

Athletically, however, Texas A&M has more work to do. The Aggies have not won a national championship in football since 1939. Remaining competitive on a national scale is always important to A&M's ardent supporters.

As opposed to the fickleness of many alumni groups, the loyalty and dedication that former students show toward their school have little to do with flashy successes on the football field or basketball court. Rather, that yearning to support and stay connected to A&M has been a no-holds-barred proposition, ingrained from the time students return from Fish Camp to the moment they slip on their Aggie Ring.

One day, all the pieces will fit together, and the window for others to understand the Aggie way of life will open as wide as it did when the news of the Bonfire collapse spread worldwide. Maybe it will take another national title run in football to make the spotlight shine on the Aggies. Maybe another shocking 1998 season will unfold, or another Jarrin' John Kimbrough or John David Crow or Dat Nguyen will rise into the country's consciousness.

But one autumn, Aggie spirit and Aggie football will be recognized together as having no peers, and the secret will be out: Texas A&M really is a place like no other.

Earning a degree from A&M is a multifaceted experience of growing together under an incredible umbrella of spirit, passion, and loyalty toward something grander than yourself.

INDEX

Page numbers in *italics* refer to illustrations and captions.

Acknowledgments

Many thanks go out to a special group of people who helped make this book possible.

First, I owe the staff of the 12th Man Foundation a big thanks for all their support. To Rusty Burson, whose guidance, expertise, and friendship over the years have meant so much; to Nick McGuire, whose knowledge of and passion for Texas A&M inspired me each day; to Trey Wright, for his incredible design talents; to Reagan Chessher and Travis Dabney for those lunches that broke up the long days; and to Miles Marks, who eagerly afforded me the time and resources to pursue this dream.

And perhaps no one steered me in the right direction in search of sources and stories better than Cathy Capps of the Texas A&M Sports Museum and Lettermen's Association. I'd like to thank Gene Starner for coming up with the idea for the book and senior associate athletic director John Thornton for sending the book idea my way. Thanks to Vince Lombardi (that's his real name) and photographers Kevin Bartram and Glen Johnson for all of their work and dedication to *12th Man Magazine;* to the Sam Houston Sanders Corps of Cadets Center, University Relations, and the Texas A&M Sports News Office for their open photo files; and to John Lindsey, for being such a classy representative of Texas A&M and a historical source for the university. I also would like to salute Howard Shelton, for his love of the 1939 national champions, and Jack Finney for his perspective on the Bear Bryant days in Aggieland. Thanks to David Chapman for his extensive knowledge of A&M's storied past. And I'd like to acknowledge *Texas Monthly*'s Paul Burka and thesis writer Heidi Ann Knippa for their works that were so helpful in researching this book.

I especially thank George Bush, forty-first President of the United States, for his graciousness and support of A&M and this project.

A special debt is owed to Jerry Cox, a visionary for the future and one of the Aggies I respect the most. A belated thanks goes out to Bill Haisten, an early mentor and one of the best sportswriters I know. And this book would not exist without the enthusiasm and professionalism of editorial director Barbara Morgan, editor Fred DuBose, designer Richard Berenson, and copy editor Arlene Petzal.

Finally, salutations to Aggies everywhere, who have created this incredible Aggie spirit and made Texas A&M such an interesting and special place.

Credits

All photos by Kevin Bartram and Glen Johnson except those listed below:

Sanders Corps of Cadets Center, College Station, Texas:
Pages 13, 15, 17, 18, 20, 24, 30, 39 (top), 42–43, 124, 125, 126, 127, 128, 146, 155 (top, left), 185, 186, 187, 188–189, 190

Texas A&M Sports News Office:
Pages 20 (top), 22–23, 46, 52, 58–59, 61, 62, 63, 64, 66, 67, 69, 70–71, 72, 73, 74, 76, 77, 78, 82–83, 87, 88, 90, 193

Texas A&M Athletic Sports Museum Archives:
Pages 18 (bottom), 34, 36, 37, 40, 45, 51, 60, 86

Texas A&M University Relations: Pages 130, 131, 132, 133, 134–135, 148, 149

Aggieland Yearbook: Pages 20 (bottom, left), 26, 30

12th Man Magazine: Pages 56, 187

Texas Aggie Magazine: Page 186

Courtesy Howard Shelton: Pages 53, 55

Courtesy Judy Franklin: Pages 28, 29

©Reuters NewMedia Inc./CORBIS: Page 85 (left)

©Bettmann/CORBIS: Page 85 (right)

TEXT:

Quotations on pages 78, 79 (Vol. 4, No. 17), 84–85, 86, 87, 88, 91 (Vol. 3, No. 7), 99 (Vol. 3, No 10) from *Aggies Illustrated*

On pages 132–133, 136, 138, 145 from *Texas Aggie Magazine Bonfire Memorial Issue*

On page 13 from *Texas Monthly (April 1997)*